Comfort *for the Tears*
Light *for the Way*

Melissa Desveaux

© 2016 by Melissa Desveaux

ISBN: 978-0-9924993-3-4
All rights reserved. No part of this document may be reproduced or transmitted in any form or by any means, electronic, mechanical, photocopying, recording, or otherwise, without prior written permission from the publisher.

All photographs in this book are printed with permission and are copyright to the their owners.

Published - designed and complied by Melissa Desveaux – www.mylifeofloss.com

Cover photograph - Sally Kennedy Photography - www.facebook.com/SallyKennedyPhotography

Cover design - Kelly Tremble - www.facebook.com/MillyBooDesigns/

Formatting - Mustafa Johnson - Lolitemedia.com

Editor – Anne-Marie Emerson McDonald - Emerson Editing - proofreading and fact checking

Trigger warning:
This book contains sensitive and emotional photographs and memoirs. They are factual and are written by people who have experienced complications before, during and after pregnancy. We appreciate your respectful consideration.

Contents

Acknowledgments	6
Introduction	7
My Life of Loss	11
Please Tell Mummy	18
Fiona Kirk - Loss Taught me to Love myself	25
Janice Dufficy	35
Christine Mckenna	43
Olivia	47
Our Journey to Happiness	59
Our Precious Boys	71
Our Precious Gem - Ruby 22-11-14	79
Oliver	89
When a Pregnancy is Unwanted	93
One Heart, Thrice Broken	97
Nay-Nay, Our Early Arriver	105
Ava Grace-Birth Story	113
Our Precious Twins Complete our Family	117
The Storm after the Rainbow	123
Jayden James	137
Zak	143
Emilee	161
Seven Angels… Sette Angeli	169
The Moment Our Family Became Stronger	175
Chaunté Rose	181
Trials and Tribulations	189
Thank You	196
Support	198

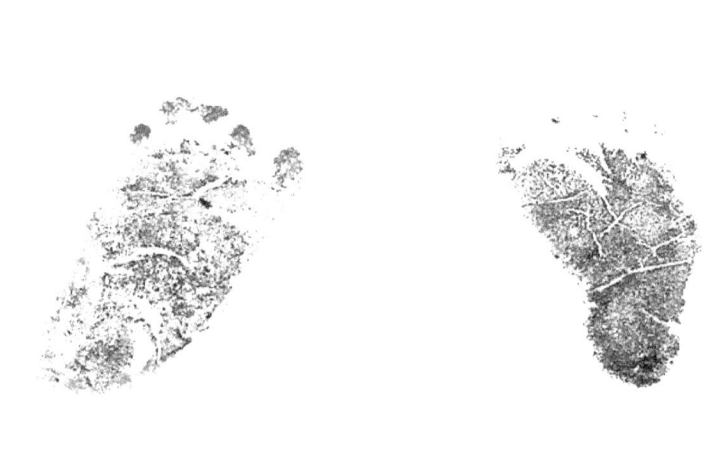

God
Didn't promise days without pain
Laughter
without sorrow
nor ## Sun without
Rain But he did promise
Strength
for the day
Comfort
for the Tears and
Light
for the way

Acknowledgments

Meredith Bale
Jeanette Buhagiar
Meekehleh Maree Connors
Janice Dufficy
Jacinta Gould
Erin and Mathew Johnson
Shalina Johnson
Fiona Kirk
Maree
Christine McKenna
Dani Milward
Natalie Panetta
Rebecca Riggio
Tara Roulston
Alicia Sinfield
Tenielle Symington
Jenny Tiernan
Martina Vassallo
Carolyn Viera
Annaleise and Kyle Williams
Rachel Windsor-Cormack

Introduction

Comfort for the Tears, Light for the Way is a collection of memoirs written by those who have endured heartache before, during and after pregnancy.

This book is inspirational. It is dedicated to anyone who needs support during the tough times of grief and loss.

These memoirs are raw and real. There is heartbreak. There is love and hope. As this book title suggests, it is comforting to know that we are not alone in this world of our grief, and there will always be a light that will guide the way.

I have been pregnant six times and two times out of those six, I was delivered of two beautiful babies. They bring me so much joy. I miscarried three pregnancies and my baby girl was born without a breath.

Before my first pregnancy, both my sisters delivered premature babies. They were left feeling overwhelmed and helpless when their babies were in the NICU for many weeks before they were allowed home.

My husband and I have not only been affected by our own grief.

We have felt heartache when our relatives and friends have experienced the loss of their babies too. These life experiences affect everyone in the circle we share.

When a baby dies at any stage of pregnancy, is born prematurely, or has been diagnosed with an illness, the impact these experiences have on their parents and families is heartbreaking. It becomes a journey for them and one they will learn to understand and live with.

My first book, *My Life of Loss*, was published in March 2014. I wrote it to help me understand my own grief. I thought it might help other parents in a similar situation.

But ever since my loss, I have envisioned a different kind of book: a collection of stories written personally by people that have experienced first-hand complications while trying to start or add to their family.

By expressing our emotions and the events that occur within our lives, by writing them down, we can find a way to release that burden. It's a healing process and a way to continue on our path.

Since *My Life of Loss* was published, I've had so many inspirational opportunities through the media to share more about my journey and my desire to help others.

I have been inspired to continue my journey in helping families find comfort and healing in the midst of grieving for the loss of a baby during or after pregnancy.

In the last two years, I have met some amazing people online and in person that have been through the journey of grief and heartache with a pregnancy that hasn't been a joyful experience.

When I gave these people the opportunity to share their heartbreaking and heartwarming pregnancy experiences too, the response I received was amazing!

Comfort for the Tears, Light for the Way is a way of giving the world an opportunity to hold onto one book, to share understanding, to show compassion and empathise with these families that have endured pregnancy struggles. Most of all, it is an opportunity to believe in hope and happiness in your own lives with an open heart and wide eyes.

Melissa Desveaux

My Life of Loss

There was nothing to suggest my second pregnancy wouldn't be normal. From my first to my last, they were everything *but* normal.

I had miscarried my first pregnancy, which was devastating and surreal, but all seemed well second time around.

When I was 18 weeks pregnant, I went to the local scanning centre for a morphology scan to check the baby's size. They told us that the baby looked small and recommended we get a in-depth scan done to be sure everything was OK.
That was when our life started to fall apart.

My doctor referred me to Sydney Ultrasound for Women to see a foetal management specialist. We were told that our baby was small for her gestational age - two weeks behind in growth.

The next few weeks were a burden. Physically and mentally my husband and I were drained, worried, anxious and scared. There really isn't a way to describe our feelings.

I had many blood tests done, including an amniocentesis to rule out any abnormalities, and they all came back normal.

I was about 21 weeks pregnant. The scans still showed little growth in our baby's development so the specialist decided to wait a week to see if there was an improvement.

At our next scan there was little. The specialist was very concerned about the health of our baby and suggested waiting another three weeks, hoping to see a dramatic change.

The long wait of three weeks finally arrived. I was in the 25th week of pregnancy - but the news hadn't improved. Our baby still hadn't grown much and the specialist advised us that the placenta was not functioning properly and our baby wasn't receiving enough nutrients or oxygen. He called it *placenta inefficiency*. He said that the baby weighed 297 grams which at that age a healthy baby should be at least 500 grams. The amniotic fluid was very low so our baby couldn't move around as much as she should.
The specialist advised us to either terminate the pregnancy or just let nature take its course.

We were devastated! After one miscarriage, I wasn't prepared to lose another baby.
Our specialist told us that if our baby grew to about 600 grams by week 30 we might have a chance of early delivery by c-section.
We left with heavy hearts all the way home. There was nothing we could do - it was all up to our baby.

Our next scan at the 27th week showed there was no fluid in the sac and the baby now only weighed 320 grams. It seemed unlikely our baby would grow 300 grams in the next three weeks.
Our specialist told us that there was no chance our baby would survive. He said that the baby was too small to be delivered and in a couple of weeks her heart would just stop beating. He offered to see me every week to check the baby's progress.

Although we had prior warning, the pain and agony of knowing our baby would not survive was unbearable. We were hoping for some sort of miracle.

The night before our next appointment with our doctor, I used a Doppler to check our baby's heartbeat. It was 152 beats per minute. The next morning, I checked the heartbeat again. There was nothing. I was a little worried, and suspected that today may be the day that would change our life.

During the doctor's appointment, the ultrasound confirmed no heartbeat. "It looks like the baby has already passed, love" were the doctor's words. I was not shocked and in fact I was quite calm. He then checked my cervix.. After us asking, our doctor told us that our baby is a little girl.

Leaving our doctor, we then called our parents, gave them the news and said that we were on our way to the hospital to keep an eye on my blood pressure and to prepare for being induced the next morning. Our whole family came to see us that night.

After a concoction of medication and being induced for the next 24 hours, I started to labour. I was in extreme pain.
The midwife checked my cervix and I was dilated about 3cm at that point. My husband stayed up with me until about 3am to give me gas, then went to sleep while I was resting. I couldn't move and had to stay in one position all night with pain in my lower back.

At around 7.30am on 27 June, 2008 I was taken back to my room and our doctor came in at about 8am. He checked my cervix again. I was in a lot of pain at that point. He asked me to push a few times and our baby, a little girl, was born at 8.08am. We named her Charlize. The placenta came out a few minutes later and the pain in my back was completely gone.

There was no sound in the room. My husband was in shock and the midwife was weeping as she watched Charlize being born.

My little baby girl lay lifeless in front of me. As I sat up to see her, all I could feel at that moment was sorrow.

After Charlize was bathed, the midwife brought her back to us. I held her in my arms and kissed her forehead. She was so little.

The midwife took prints of Charlize's feet and hands and we were given a teddy bear, blanket, beanie and booties.
A priest came in to bless Charlize. Our hearts ached as we gently held her for only a short while. Then we were told our beautiful little baby needed to be taken for an autopsy. At that moment I realised she could not stay with us. The tears flowed, and I was a mess!

We left the hospital without our little baby the same afternoon. We went home to cry. We went home to sleep and not want to wake up!

Looking back, I wish I had taken photos with her that day and stayed with her longer. All I have are memories and feelings of sadness which will stay with me forever. Charlize became an angel on the 25th of July. Just one day before my grandfather passed away five years earlier and born the day after. I am sure he was looking after her and watching over me.

We started preparing her funeral the day after. This was not something we thought about. We didn't know what she would wear, what her coffin would look like, what flowers we should have, what music we should play. Nothing. But we had a few days to think about it.

We bought her a pink teddy bear blanket to keep her warm. Then chose beautiful music for her service, a white coffin and white and pink flowers. These were not meant to be a choice. Choosing to have a funeral was not in our plans for her.

Her funeral was held 3 July 2008. I was sick to my stomach and so anxious to hold my baby in my arms for the last time and say goodbye. My husband and I and a few family members held her for as long as we could. We put a little dress over her that were given to us and then covered her with our pink teddy bear blanket. I was heartbroken. I took a few photos of her - but only one with me holding her.

After a beautiful but emotional service, we left the chapel and gathered at the cemetery where Charlize was to be buried. We each placed a pink rose on her coffin. I cried and cried.
Then, in a matter of moments, she was gone.

The days that followed were filled with tears. I cried uncontrollably every time I thought about my little Charlize, knowing that I would never be able to hold her, kiss her or feed her like I should have.

For many months I grieved and, to this day, I continually think of her, wondering what our lives would have been with her a part of it.

Six weeks after her birth, we were given the results of Charlize's autopsy. They found blood clots in her brain and she was undernourished.

Although we were heartbroken, we wanted a baby to fill our hearts with joy and after a few months, I fell pregnant. I miscarried that pregnancy again in June 2009. I was sad, angry and confused. But I tried to remain positive and took from the fact I actually could fall pregnant.

On 23 July, 2010, after an induction and an emergency cesarean, I gave birth to Damien, our rainbow baby. He was 38 weeks and four days at birth. He was distressed from the umbilical cord wrapped around his neck, but this birth had a happy ending.
Our hearts melted and we were in awe with him when we saw him for the first time. We found unconditional love and are truly blessed. He is our little miracle.

Throughout this pregnancy I was injecting myself daily with Clexane, which is a medication to assist with blood clotting. I was worried everyday that something would happen and just hoped my baby would be healthy.

When Damien was 18 months old, I was diagnosed with epilepsy; causing pressure on my life as a mother and my ability to drive myself around just to go shopping with my baby on my own become a task on its own. I became dependent on others; often feeling the loss of freedom. I was subscribed life long medication which could risk to for future pregnancies.

In 2011, I again fell pregnant and again I miscarried after eight weeks. It was a stab in the heart, and again we were left disappointed and heartbroken.
I was an emotional wreck! I could not deal with my grief and care for a young child. We took it easy and went away for a couple of days.

In January 2013, I fell pregnant with my little Ethan. During the pregnancy, I was again required to have Clexane injections daily and I started the pregnancy with progesterone to facilitate the growth of the embryo.

Due to low amniotic fluid, at 38 weeks and four days, I was given the option to have another caesarian, have some testing done or wait over the weekend to see if I would go into labour naturally. I decided on the caesarian so I wouldn't risk my baby's life. Ethan was born the exact same day I miscarried a year earlier - 27 September 2013. I truly believe my angels were with me.

Although I will always grieve over the loss of my babies, I believe in miracles. My two boys are my proof. They have fulfilled my life and given me love, joy and happiness. They are my world and my hope.

My life would not be the same without having my angels to guide me. They have shown me to appreciate life; and love more.

(This memoir is a brief of my book *My Life of Loss*)

Melissa Desveaux - Southwest Sydney, Australia
www.Mylifeofloss.com

Please Tell Mummy

Mr. Jesus, please tell Mummy, I hate seeing her this way
And please make sure my Mummy doesn't continually relive that day

It wasn't meant a date of importance, until my tiny little body was born
And now the 21st of October, is a day that Mummy and Daddy will mourn

Please tell Mummy I felt her cuddles, Mr. Jesus tell her so
three beautiful long days with her and Daddy, meant more than they'll ever know

Mr. Jesus my Mummy prayed to you, I know you heard her prayers
So can you please tell Mummy, that you needed me upstairs?

Mummy and Daddy felt life was going to plan, Big brother Luca would pat Mummy's tummy in awe
But their lives have turned upside down, and Luca doesn't talk to me anymore

Poor Mummy got an infection, Mr. Jesus no one knew
Please tell my Mummy it wasn't her fault, There was nothing that she could do

It was painful to watch poor Mummy cry, that shouldn't happen to any mother
Mr. Jesus please help Mummy and Daddy be there for one another

Mr. Jesus please tell Mummy, I'm grateful for how my features were
My little fingers and pretty big feet that I inherited just from her

Mr. Jesus mummy blamed herself as she held my body so frail
Please be sure to tell Mummy that her body didn't fail

Tenielle Symington

Angel Gowns Australia

After reading an article about Angel Gowns Australia, I was deeply touched. It's an organisation that transforms donated wedding dresses to beautiful gowns for babies and infants that have left us too soon.

This organisation inspired me so much that, in August 2014, I decided to donate my own wedding dress. I also donated most of the money I made through my first book to Angel Gowns Australia.

After being contacted by the founder, Fiona Kirk, my life really has changed. She allowed me to speak from the heart at their first anniversary event (a nerve-wracking thing for me to do in front of a crowd of 100+ people!), and to take part in their first pregnancy and infant loss Remembrance Day ceremony.
I was invited to join her and her volunteers in February 2016 for a media interview. It wonderful to watch these ladies make the beautiful gowns they are known for. I could see how much love and dedication they put into making them.
I also attended their second annual gala dinner held in Melbourne (April 2016).

Fiona has helped me incredibly and I have much admiration for her. I am in awe of the love she has for Angel Gowns Australia and all the volunteers who work tirelessly to make those heartfelt and beautiful baby gowns. I am privileged to have met her and some of the volunteers. I'm honoured that some of the volunteers have shared their own stories in this book too.

Thank you for giving me these opportunities.

www.AngelgownsAustralia.org.au

Fiona Kirk
Loss Taught me to Love myself

Founder of Angel Gowns Australia

By the time you reach three years old you have been shaped by your surroundings and your dominant personality is set in place. Yes, you are born with inherent characteristics, those that will help you respond to some of the familial, environmental and structural surrounds of where you live, and ultimately the friends you meet and the experiences that life presents you. All of these things add to your life experience and the building of your character. The building of who you are today.

My inherent characteristic, the one that dominates my instincts and every action and reaction in life, is love. Sometimes I display this as love; sometimes love manifests as frustration or anger. But love is always responsible. Some would say that I am far too loving, and this indeed shaped my today and not always in a positive way. At least, not until I came to understand what love truly is.

Being someone who is so loving, I trusted those I shouldn't, often falling hard, having to scrape my squashed little heart off the pavement with a makeshift spatula, but guess what? I did it! But not without the most harrowing loss of my life: I terminated the *one* thing I always wanted, my incredibly loved and very wanted baby. I can see you now. You have a look of disbelief and dismay on your face, and quite possibly have lowered this book towards your lap, maybe closed it for now, because you have experienced 'true' loss and just cannot bear to read any more. Or maybe you are shaking your head, albeit gently, side to side and asking, Why? Or maybe you are sitting there with tears burning in your eyes because you know exactly how I feel, how I have felt every day for the past 16 years.

Many wonder why, if she is so full of love, why would she terminate the one thing she always wanted?

Let's go back to when I was eight years old. My teacher's name was Mrs. Wriggle. (Yes, you read that correctly: Wriggle. Oh my giddy aunt, I can tell you all the children use to wriggle and giggle. Children are so innocent sometimes, but a teacher with the name 'Wriggle' looking after primary school children would have to have been prepared for the giggles to the wriggles.)

Close your eyes for me and imagine Mrs. Wriggle sitting in a child's metal framed, wooden seat and backed chair, with her hands placed politely on her closed knees as she questioned the children in front of her. "Children, quiet now please". There was silence. "I would like you all to have a think about what you would like to be when you grow up." With excitement, one by one, each child stood up. "I want to be a policeman!" exclaimed Bobby "I want to be a fireman," said Peter. "I want to be a nurse," said Sally. "A vet," said Samantha. I quietly stood up, I felt my heart beating hard and my face burning red, I pushed my chest out proudly and said, "I just want to be the best mummy and the best wife in the whole wide world."

Now I am 46 and it's 2016. After that terrible day when I terminated my baby I was never given that gift of a tiny life again, my belly never grew with the most precious gift of humankind, I never counted my baby's fingers and toes, I was never blessed with a child born of my own flesh and blood. I could try to explain to you why; but sadly I just can't change what I did. I can't change what is in the past and writing about it can only place blame and I have no blame. But I can share with you how I felt before and how I felt after losing my baby.

When I realised I was pregnant, I felt different, like I had been awakened. I thought clearer, heard clearer, saw clearer. I got dressed to go to work and couldn't understand what I was feeling. It was strange but curious.

When I stepped out the front door on to the footpath, the buildings in front of me were so beautiful, like I was seeing them for the first time! The trees so green, the birds chirping louder than I had ever heard before and as I walked up the road I felt a childish giggle bubble up... I felt so happy, yet I didn't know why.

I then said, "Oh - my - goodness… I am pregnant!" I immediately rang work and said I was unable to come in, then went to the chemist and bought a pregnancy test. Before I knew it I was staring at two beautiful pinkish-red lines on the pregnancy strip… I was pregnant!! Oh my goodness! The feeling of joy was incredible, and then just as quickly the darkness hit because I knew he wouldn't want this baby, and I felt sick, so I tried to keep it a secret for as long as I could, even planning to leave him if I had to.

My pregnancy was so very unplanned and I knew he wouldn't want our baby. I prayed for two weeks that he would. I kept my baby a secret from everyone, safe inside, roots taking hold. I wanted to keep my baby safe so he could not make me terminate the precious life I had already grown so much to love; I was already so in love with the tiny precious blue eyed soul inside me.

The day I lost my baby – yes, to me I lost my baby - was around 3:30pm on 19 April, 2000. I was a broken young woman who felt so alone in this world. I was given jellybeans, of all things, when I woke up – the shape of a tiny 8 week gestational fetus; I knocked them to the floor, rolled over and prayed I would wake up from this terrible nightmare. I went home to die.

I thought I went home to a promised life of changes from the man I thought loved me, but I knew by the look on his face that nothing was going to change. So I lay in bed curled up in a ball waiting for day seven because I had heard that you die of starvation and dehydration if you don't eat or drink for seven days. I lay there not eating and not drinking; just lying there praying to the gods that they would just take me away, I just wanted to start life over again. I wanted my baby back.

On the seventh day I had what might be called an out of body experience. I felt my old favourite dog, Sheba – who died a few years earlier - walk up on my bed, bit by bit, in her old playful way. She was a big Rhodesian Ridgeback, so she was very noticeable. I felt her walk up behind me, walk one way in a circle then the other way and, after a few repeats of this, she finally laid down and placed her heavy head on my neck in between my chin and my shoulder. I felt her warm breath on my face. I fell into a deep, calm, peaceful sleep. I knew I was going to die and Sheba had come to guide me. I felt so incredibly happy that I was going to play with her again and meet the soul of the baby taken from me.

I obviously didn't die, but I left that relationship and since have found out what true love really is. And that started with loving who I was and not trying to be what everyone else wanted me to be, or what I perceived they wanted me to be.

Life has not been easy. Life is never meant to be easy.
Almost 10 years later I met my husband, Travis Kirk, in 2009. He came with three children: his stepson Aden, who is half-brother to Nathan and Zachary, Travis' two younger sons. Together, we make the most perfect family, often spending time with the children's mum who is a very important person in all of our lives. I complete this special extended family.
It was with the harrowing loss of my only baby, many mistakes, finding myself and meeting the love of my life, I was able to do what I was put on this earth to do - give and share love.

Starting Angel Gowns Australia was a natural step in my life's journey; my journey to Angel Gowns Australia.

I've always loved fundraising, ever since my very first experience, when I was 14, innocent and naïve about processes and law. This is a fond memory actually. I was watching TV early on a Saturday morning; it was a telethon for the Royal Melbourne Children's Hospital's Easter Appeal, raising money for sick children. I wanted to donate some money to them but I only had $2.

So I made a plan to have a raffle at the local shopping centre. With my $2, I purchased a raffle book and started approaching people explaining that I was raising money to give to the Easter Appeal, and the prize would be a gigantic chocolate Easter bunny. I snuck out of my bedroom window on late night shopping nights and surprisingly people purchased tickets without seeing the prize and without seeing any identification. How I managed to raise $3,000 I can't tell you; but I do know I was having fun and feeling very chuffed with the money I had raised for those sick children I felt so very sad for. I had nothing other than the best intentions.

The next person I approached turned out to be a policeman - remember, I didn't think I was doing anything wrong - so I tried to sell him a ticket. In no time at all I was at the police station and shaking in my socks, actually I was so scared I was truly trembling! I was given a hot chocolate and piece of cake, asked a lot of questions and could see a lot of the police officers looking at me, however curiously they seemed to be giggling. Then my Dad arrived and everything changed! I was in trouble and there was no more hot chocolate and cake for me! We put all the tickets in a waste paper basket, drew a ticket out and rang the winner. The police went and purchased a massive chocolate Easter bunny and the rest was donated to where I wanted it to go. I was sent home; deep down I was so happy but I knew I was grounded and in big, big trouble!

I have since volunteered for a number of children's charities, and always raised and donated money where I could. In 2012 I ran an event for Habitat for Humanity, High Tea in the Capital. This was a very successful event with over 200 people attending, three fashion shows, three dance shows and market stalls.

In 2014 I started my own charity. I was following a page on Facebook, "Isabelle Rose, our precious hero", a tiny baby girl diagnosed at only four weeks of age with infantile leukemia. This baby girl put up the biggest fight, smiling through so much pain in her tiny body, but sadly lost her battle at eight months of age on the 26th of March, 2014.

From this page I was, I believe, guided to an article on an Angel Gown program in America run by Lisa Grubbs, called NICU Helping Hands – Angel Gown Program. This program made tiny Angel Gown garments from donated wedding dresses. An internet and social media search showed there were no programs like this in Australia, so before 9pm on the 27th of March I started Angel Gowns Australia and took my first pledged wedding dresses. My own blush rose-coloured wedding dress was also cut up and the first Angel Gown garment named "The Isabella Rose", was sent to her parents. All I hoped was that that gown would give just one moment of peace and beauty to them, knowing that I cared.

I believe that everything that had happened in my life up to that point had been leading me to Angel Gowns Australia.
I was joined by a number of amazing women, some of whom are still with the organisation two years on. Being the founder of Angel Gowns Australia gives me, and will always give me incredible pride and honour in what I achieved personally, especially realising my dream to run my own children's charity. However, with my heart on my sleeve my deepest pride lays with all of the volunteers who have worked just as hard as I have to build the foundations, to set the highest of standards and to make sure that the reputation and future of Angel Gowns Australia would always be loved, admired and talked about.

With the love and commitment of Angel Gowns Australia's volunteers we have ensured thousands of families each year when faced with the death of their baby receive the precious gift on an Angel Gown garment, giving them support and reassuring them they are not alone and that the greater community cares about them and their baby.

If you get a really big jigsaw puzzle of a heart with a background of the most beautiful blue sky, you will find that each puzzle piece inside the heart is one of us, each puzzle piece from the heart has a name and that name belongs to one of the volunteers; a seamstress, a manager, representative, administration, committee member, deconstructor, packer, no matter what they do, each piece of the puzzle is the same size, just shaped differently, just as all of our skills are different. And just like a puzzle, each piece fits into the next to create a beautiful picture. All of our skills lock together in our puzzle with each of us becoming the heartbeat of Angel Gowns Australia.

Each blue piece of the sky has a name on it, each piece belongs to those who support us, our followers, our sponsors and all of the selfless brides who have donated their wedding dress. If you look really close, if you look long enough you will see the names of all our precious babies rising above this puzzle. They are the names of all of our precious babies taken far too soon.

Angel Gowns Australia works because "We believe in the healing ability of giving and sharing; of love, compassion and community." Our volunteers are the most important aspect of our programs and we would not be able to function without them.
We have over 340 volunteers made up of women who have experienced the loss of their own baby, family and friends who were affected by the loss of a baby, and mothers and fathers who simply cannot imagine how other families feel after losing their baby and want to help in any way they can; and of course all of our wonderful businesses who are supporting us and coming together to make sure we can supply our Angel Gown garments to families, hospitals and funeral homes all around Australia at absolutely no charge.

Our Angel Gown garments are in hospitals and funeral homes all around Australia. We have Angel Gown garments ready at all times, because we know how precious time is when a baby dies. However, we also have the option, when a baby dies, for the family to contact us for any special requirements. We never say no, and we make sure we deliver our Angel Gown garments within 48 hours where possible. We also arrange to pick up the mother's wedding dress, create their precious Angel Gown garment and arrange to send it back to the family so they can dress their baby.

We have a very precious saying at Angel Gowns Australia, something I wrote with Katrina Sheraton-Yu (our then vice president and a very dear friend), late at night:
"We hope to give each family just one moment of peace and beauty as they dress their baby, spending precious time together before they have to say goodbye for the very last time."

I received a letter from a lady who had had a miscarriage; she wanted to share her story with me. She mentioned in her letter that she felt her loss was not seen to be the same to that of other women who had lost babies after 20 weeks gestation, especially full term babies. I wrote back to her and what I wrote has now also become part of who we are and how we feel about pregnancy, baby and infant loss:

"It is often difficult for people to understand when a baby dies, no matter how early or late in gestation, that the life of that baby has already been celebrated as a mother and a father, and then celebrated with family and friends, imprinted into our hearts and souls. When losing this tiny life there is so much grief and heartache, the same grief and heartache of any parent, of any family when a life is lost."

When a special order comes in for one of our precious tiny Angels taken far too soon, something incredible happens.
We have a private communication page where all of our volunteers chat together, giving advice and sharing stories, pictures of the Angel Gown garments they create and giving each other support. It is here we put up communication that a baby has died and we need help from the closest seamstress and volunteers to make this happen overnight.

No matter how late it is many of the volunteers pull together to organise who is going to do the sewing, who can pick up the wedding dress and who is going to deliver the gown to the family when made. It is a magical experience, watching how everything is done and how quickly. Yes, there is always heartache behind the busy activity; but it's also incredibly heartwarming because not one question is asked by these volunteers - they just do. I can only imagine that this is what heaven would look like when something is needed to be done, with love, care and gentleness.

I had always wanted to run my own children's charity, but I never imagined it would be for the most precious time in a child's life: their final goodbye.

I was meant to bring love into this world, and I did.

Fiona Kirk - Canberra, Australia

Janice Dufficy

Volunteer for Angel Gowns Australia

When you are pregnant, you fantasize about the sex of the baby, the hopes and anticipation of what this new life will mean, and the joy of bringing of a new life into the world to be loved and cherished by you, your husband, family and friends.

To have experienced the losses that many of the women in this book have known is beyond my comprehension.

I feel so lucky. I had two uneventful lovely pregnancies, and had two healthy children – my daughter Leah (31), and son Tom (27). I have my wonderful husband of 38 years, Terry, who is loving and supportive of all my activities. We also have an amazing extended family.

I'd like to share with you some of the voluntary work I've done over the years, particularly my commitment to join Angel Gowns Australia as a volunteer seamstress.

Casting my mind back, I think my interest in volunteer work started when I was a Sunday School teacher at the age of 14, at St. David's Church of England Church, in Greenacre. After finishing school I worked for a while, but when my children were small I undertook the following voluntary roles:

- On the church cleaning roster for Menai Uniting Church;
- Day leader for Playgroup;
- Secretary of Menai Occasional Child Care Centre (5 years+);
- Various activities at Menai Primary School – tutor reading programme, canteen, covering many library books etc;
- At Menai Hawks Soccer Club, I was manager over the years of various teams, and took on the role of canteen co-ordinator at one of the three fields operated by the club – namely Casuarina Oval (8+ years);
- And any other duties as required!

Most recently, following a request I viewed on Facebook from Sutherland Shire Carers' Support Service, I am now assisting a disabled young man to do his voluntary work at Sutherland Shire Council in the Children's Services Section. This is a new role for me, and one I am committed to. It may be interesting to learn that when I discovered who this young man was, he was someone special who I knew well. I first met him and his mother when I had my daughter Leah, 31 years ago in St. George Hospital. We were both in the same hospital after giving birth to our first child. Both children went to the same playgroup, primary school and were in the same soccer team!

When my daughter Leah married her partner, Amanda, in Portugal in 2013, they then went down the path of donor sperm from the United States to conceive a child.

It was successful and little Luke was born in April 2014. My boss at the time gave me the day off and as a new grandmother, I received flowers for doing nothing – Amanda did all the hard work! How nice!

Prior to the birth of Luke, I embarked on my crocheting passion, making heaps of unusual things in anticipation of Luke's arrival and posting photos of my creations on Facebook.

One day I had lunch with a group of long-time friends, most of whom had seen these photos. One of these dear friends, Kerrie Jones, suggested that I make contact with a new organisation known as Angel Gowns Australia , thinking that they may want me to make crocheted items for them.

I pursued this via email and received a reply stating that crocheting wasn't required but that dressmaking was.

I thought about this for a while, as I hadn't sewn for a few years, and didn't know whether my old Janome machine could be resurrected or function without encouragement, and I had reservations about my ability.

My faithful Janome, who is behaving, and my dining room taken over with my sewing for Angel Gown Australia.
I am not a professional sewer, but have always loved sewing given the time. I have re-covered lounges, drafted patterns, sewn beautiful dresses in my younger days, made curtains, embroidered etc. I did rather well in year 10 quite a few decades ago, and my School Certificate results put me in the top 10 per cent in New South Wales.

After thinking about this new commitment, I decided to give it a go. I filled in the necessary forms, submitted my sample gowns and lo and behold – I was accepted! My phone rang hot as I posted this on my Facebook page and couldn't wait to get started.
I will never forget receiving my first wedding gown to work on when I attended an open day at Engadine Community Centre in January 2015.

I burst through the front door when I arrived home, full of enthusiasm to show my husband. I then spent hours thinking of what I was going to do with it, particularly when I realised how special this gown was to the bride on her wedding day and how important her donation was.

As I made my first cut on the gown, the significance of my commitment to Angel Gowns Australia became very real and confronting. I had to do my very best, be creative and make garments symbolic of the wedding gown. However, this can be difficult as, depending on the gown, you are sometimes limited.

Also, our clientele – hospitals Australia-wide and our major sponsor, Guardian Funerals – have requested that our gowns be simple and unisex when possible. As most of the gowns donated lend themselves to feminine creations, I have tried to focus on male garments.

With my first gown, I knew the name and details of the donor. The first thing I made was a keepsake for the bride, incorporating a design that was symbolic of her gown. The photograph pictured shows the heart cushion I made depicting the lace over the satin, and then using the gathered lace from her train, I surrounded the heart with it.

I posted it off with a note of thanks to the bride with my details, and shortly after received a wonderful personal phone call thanking me and advising she had been in touch with her relatives following receipt of her keepsake.

If my records are correct, I am about to embark on gown 11.
The heart keepsake I made for the donor bride, a sleeping bag with vest, bonnet and wrap is pictured.

When I reflect on my past and my family history, I realise where my need and desire to join Angel Gowns Australia came from.
My grandmothers and my mother both lost little girls – my grandmother Ethel Maud Ingle-Olson (Brady) lost two-year-old Beryl; my other grandmother Gwendoline Maud Mafeking Johnston (Marshall) lost nine-month-old Anne; and my mother Enid Gwendoline

Ingle-Olson (Johnston), lost my sister three-week-old Jill, and also found her sister Anne 'asleep' when she was a young girl.
All these bereaved mothers were told to "just get on with it" and forget their losses. It was never acknowledged or discussed and they endured their grief silently, constantly and sadly. My wonderful Mum, now 88, recently cried, yet again, when I asked her about their losses.

Mum loves what I do for Angel Gowns Australia and acknowledges this, but says that she wished I were doing something for the living. Mum doesn't realise that our Angels are still living – in our hearts always.

Mum still thinks differently and still suffers her loss as if it was yesterday. I love Mum dearly. She says the truth and is incredibly honest, loving and supportive.

Thank goodness for Angel Gowns Australia. It has given me, as a volunteer, purpose, love, support, enduring friendships and the opportunity to spend my time doing something voluntary for a community who needs this service.

As a volunteer over many years and genres, I have unexpectedly received benefits that I had no idea I would experience. Long-standing friendship is a very special one; plus the huge personal satisfaction that my efforts have, in some way, maybe made a difference.

On a silly note, I went to the hairdressers today and was talking about my wonderful adventures. My hairdresser, Sonya, said that she has wealthy friends who are bored. Well why aren't they volunteering! They surely have the time and talent to do something for others, so why don't they embark on a new wonderful journey and experience the satisfaction of giving whatever time they can spare in one of the many facets of volunteering to suit their talent and interest? They would be welcomed with open arms.

As an amateur seamstress, sewing is what I try to do to the best of my ability. As an added bonus, sewing isn't all that is involved

when you become involved with Angel Gowns Australia.
Many Angel Gowns Australia volunteers don't know one another personally, but there are opportunities to assist in other ways and finally meet up with Angel Gowns Australia Facebook friends.
I have had the privilege of being part of working bees at Linnwood House, Guildford on various occasions, a packing day at Ryde and manning information stalls at craft shows at Rosehill, Homebush and Glebe Island. I look forward to more.

I seem to be a magnet for strange questions. At Glebe Island a lady came up to me to ask whether Angel Gowns Australia would consider making angel garments for pets! I spoke to her sympathetically, and I think I referred her to Pets at Peace.

About me:
I worked for Members of Parliament in NSW for decades, the last Member being Linda Burney, in her electorate office, finishing in August 2015.
I'm a keen Jazzerciser (over 35 years).
I play golf with the Alfords Point Ladies Social Club (15 years) – but I'm hopeless at it, however one good shot out of 18 holes ensures my return.
I obtained a Graduate Certificate in Multicultural Journalism at the University of Wollongong at around 50 years of age – proving you are never too old to learn.
I'm a Justice of the Peace.

Janice Dufficy - Sydney, Australia

Christine Mckenna

Volunteer for Angel Gowns Australia

I am a mother and a grandmother. Two of my own daughters have had three losses between them in the past seven years. My mother had three miscarriages as well. She told me you never forget.

I wanted to do something to help. I felt my skills as a dressmaker could be put to good use. To honour the babies' lives and as a "pay back" for having a successful outcome following my diagnosis with stage 3B bowel cancer in late 2013.
So I joined Angel Gowns Australia on the day it was founded, 27 March, 2014.

I am now national secretary of Angel Gowns Australia and co-chair of the organisation's seamstress and creative committee. I am also a board member and serve on other committees as a general member.

I have been called on to make many special requests, especially for our garments made from a family member's own wedding or debutante dress. I find it particularly rewarding to do this, even though knowing that a particular little Angel will wear one of my creations is often so heartbreaking.

Last year I was asked to make the pink blanket [pictured] for Lily Grace, a little baby who was found abandoned in the dunes at Maroubra Beach and was buried by the local community who rallied to mark her passing. The keepsake heart was given to the lady who organised the service as a thank you gesture.

I really feel very honoured to be making tributes to lost babies. It is such a gift, knowing that I am making a difference in a bereaved family's life. We often get such heartfelt thank you letters from recipients of our Angel Gown garments and wraps, and we read every one of them with pride.

                Christine Mckenna - Sydney Australia

"This was not the birth I expected. I expected to hold my baby and cry happy tears. I was exhausted, confused, scared and lost"

Olivia

My daughter Olivia was born at 33 weeks and four days' gestation. There was no medical reasoning or conclusion as to why she arrived early, all we were told was that there had been a premature rupture of the membranes.

My daughter's due date was 2 July, 2014. We were in the process of renovating our home while we were pregnant with her. I never really did a thing to help as my husband wouldn't let me! He said it was too hard for me and I had to rest. But my pregnancy was smooth sailing; my blood pressure and blood tests were always perfect; no gestational diabetes; absolutely no issues whatsoever.

I was excited for my baby shower, which was to be held on Saturday, 17 May. Two days before, I was out shopping with my mum getting everything we needed. I started to feel exhausted while we were out and we had to end our shopping trip early.

Later that night I had a really uncomfortable feeling between my legs. It felt like a big bulge was sitting there and I was aching from head to toe. It almost felt like I hadn't sat down in days. My husband sent me to bed with a cup of warm tea and told me to watch TV and not to move.

The next morning I had my midwife appointment, and the midwife I saw was not my usual one. However, the student midwife who had been with me the whole journey so far was there. I explained everything I had been feeling and the midwife said I was 100 per cent fine, the baby was nowhere near ready, and they would see me back for my next appointment in two weeks. Boy, were they wrong!

My baby shower was held the following day. I was beyond tired, a feeling I have never felt before. Most of my guests stayed well past the finish time. I was emotional and completely drained. I broke down in tears and said to my sister, "All I want to do is rest. Could you please nicely ask the remaining guests if they could leave?" A finish time that was meant to be 4pm turned into guests not leaving until 9pm! I had a cool shower and went to bed once everyone left.

The following morning I woke up and felt awful. I remained in bed and slept most of the day. On the Monday I felt a little bit better. I thought I would start to pack my hospital bags - task that soon proved too tiring and made me quickly sit down. I was back to feeling overly exhausted. I started feeling very anxious and stressed about cleaning, and even though I was tired all I wanted to do was scrub my kitchen and prepare dinner.

Later that night I had a warm shower and when I got out, I blow-dried my hair. In the process I felt a trickle down my leg and my pyjama pants were drenched. I knew I hadn't wet myself; it was a different feeling to passing urine. It was uncontrollable. It would start then stop and start again. I yelled out to my husband and told him to ring the hospital. We told the nurses that I was only at 33 weeks gestation, to which they advised me to put a maternity pad on and come in immediately.

A trip to the hospital that took 10 minutes felt like half an hour. Once we arrived we went straight into the birthing suite. I wasn't feeling any pain, just losing more and more fluid. The nurses sent us into the assessment room and checked the fluid I was losing and confirmed active labour. They had neonatal doctors see us and also other doctors, whose job was to monitor me if anything went wrong.
There was no real explanation as to why our baby was coming early. There was no turning back. No keeping her in. She was coming!

I was given a steroid injection in my backside to help with our baby's lung development. This was to be given to me again in another 12 hours if I hadn't given birth to her by then. The nurses completed an internal to check if I had dilated at all. I was 1cm. The doctors advised us that we had to prepare for the worst, however we didn't really understand their medical jargon. They said that in most cases babies born at this gestation were OK, however sometimes things can go wrong and they don't make it. It depended on the baby itself.

As I didn't have pain I was sent to the antenatal ward. My husband had to leave for the night, as he wasn't allowed to stay. They said they would phone him if he were needed. I've never been so scared in my life. All I wanted at that point was my husband. Between the other patients snoring, strange noises, a dark room, being scared, losing more fluid and having to pass urine every 5-10 minutes, I had no sleep. Around 3am I started getting sharp menstrual-like pains in my stomach and asked the nurses for pain relief. They went to get it but never returned. There was a shift change and the previous nurse forgot to advise the current nurse that I needed meds.

Hours passed and I couldn't handle the pain, I asked for pain relief again and told the nurses that the pain was getting worse. They did another internal and I was 3cm dilated. The nurses decided it was time to go to the birthing suite. All I could think of was my husband. I needed him. He arrived about 9.30am. The date was now Tuesday, 20 May - a day I can never forget.

I received my second steroid injection at 10am. The midwife suggested I start taking the gas for pain relief because I started to become uncomfortable. It worked right away, but it didn't last long. Soon I was having continuous contractions without a gap in between, and the midwife suggested I receive an epidural as I wasn't getting a break. I was struggling to breathe. My daughter's heart rate was increasing and I was told that she could become distressed. The anesthetist came to speak with me and receive my consent for the needle. But I was in so much pain that I couldn't focus, so I couldn't talk to him. He asked the nurses to check my dilation because he was sure I was too far gone for an epidural. He was correct.

The midwife told me to open my legs and to her surprise our daughter was crowning! I remember hearing sirens and strange emergency noises. The machines were going crazy! I could barely open my eyes but I could faintly see a whole team of people surrounding a big crane-like machine. A female doctor wearing blue scrubs held my hand and talked in my ear, saying, "Only focus on my voice and listen to everything I tell you to do." This woman with her calm, caring manner was my saviour! She was heaven sent and helped me so much. To this day I have no idea who she was but I salute her.

After a few pushes and many screams, our little girl was out. Born at 12.47pm, weighing 2.008kg and 47cm long. She didn't cry as she wasn't breathing. They rushed her to the big crane machine and a whole team of doctors worked on her. All I could do was cry and ask if she was OK. She had tubes everywhere and breathing apparatus on her face. She was rushed out of the room. I told my husband to not worry about me but to stay with our daughter.
This was not the birth I expected. I expected to hold my baby and cry happy tears. I was exhausted, confused, scared and lost. The midwife delivered the placenta and told me everything was fine and that I did well.

A room full of people soon attended to me. A midwife came back in and told me to try and have a rest and then they would come back in an hour and get me up for a shower. After an hour my husband came back to birthing suite. He had photos of our little girl and said she was fine but needed help with breathing. The midwife asked if I felt OK to try and get up to have a shower. All I wanted to do was have one! I felt terrible.

Trying to get up off the bed proved difficult and it was very challenging as after birth began to seep out. My husband being the amazing person he is stayed with me the entire time in the shower so I didn't fall, as I began to feel dizzy. After my shower the midwife organised a sandwich and a drink for me to give me some energy. They asked me once I finished eating to grab my bags and to sit in the wheelchair and they would take me to see my daughter.

In the meantime, my husband's family had arrived. They were extremely excited to see their new addition. She was the first grandchild on my husband's side and the first granddaughter on my side.

When we arrived at NICU I realised the seriousness of my daughter's situation. Visitors to the unit were limited and no children were allowed in at all. Even though I was taken aback by the strict rules, I was extremely grateful that the number one priority was the babies. People were kept out to give these vulnerable babies a chance at life.

The room was dark. Ten machines held 10 babies. My husband wheeled me to our daughter. My first thought was, She's so tiny. Machines and tubes covered her little face and body. Tears rolled down my cheeks. This is the little person who was inside me for all of these months kicking me and keeping me awake all night. I longed to touch her and as I went to put my hand through the holes in the machine, I was advised not to by a NICU nurse. She said she was far too young and fragile to be touched. Stimulation could increase her heart rate.

I felt like all my rights as her mother were taken away. Being a first-time mum I already had no idea what to expect but this was a completely unexpected situation. I was then wheeled up to postnatal and given a room. I lay down for a while and then asked my husband to take me down to see our baby again. My heart was pounding like a little child getting excited over an amusement park. I was so anxious and excited to see our baby - I just felt like running there rather than being wheeled down in a wheelchair.

When we got to the NICU security doors, we were asked for our child's name and the doors were unlocked. There she was - our little princess, sleeping peacefully but still covered in tubes and machines. Never had I seen anything so pure and beautiful in my life.

A lovely nurse introduced herself to us. She said her name was Philippa and she would be looking after our daughter overnight. A sense of relief came over me because I knew she was in good hands. Philippa said, "I know you want to sit here all night and stare at her but I can tell you're extremely tired. Can I suggest you get some sleep? You can come down any time during the night if you wake up."

My husband said she was right and there was nothing we could do for our baby. She couldn't feed, couldn't be held. There was no point me being there. All I asked was that if she woke up or cried could they please call me so I can be there. Philippa agreed.

Going up to my room again made me feel like a piece of me was missing, but I managed to get some sleep. I woke during the night and had to request some pain relief as I started to feel cramps. As soon as the medication kicked in I was comfortable and got some more sleep. Even though I was waking every 2-3 hours I felt OK and somewhat relaxed.

The next day I got up to freshen myself up a little before my husband arrived. I thought I would go down by myself to see our daughter before he got there. This tiny baby laying there so helpless, made me realise how blessed I was to have been given the chance to create such a beautiful little gift.

The nurse came over to me to tell me that her heart rate had dropped overnight but was OK now.. Her temperature had also dropped so they had to alter the machines to better incubate her. When my husband arrived I told him what I had been told. He couldn't stop taking photos, he was just so proud of his baby. The nurse asked if we wanted to touch her and I felt a rush of joy that I could finally make physical contact with my baby. The little hand sections on the machine were opened and we were told not to stroke her but to place our hands on her back so she could feel us. I felt instant warmth. Then a miracle happened: our daughter opened her eyes and looked at us for the first time. Once again a tear or two rolled down my cheeks.

I went back up to my room only to be told I was being discharged. My heart sank. I wasn't ready to go home while my baby was in NICU. But the nurses said they needed the bed. I quickly went back down to NICU to tell the nurses I had to leave but I would be back in a couple of hours.

Leaving the hospital was the hardest thing I've ever had to do. I broke down in tears as soon as I got into the car. I was heartbroken. Having to leave my baby just didn't feel right. When we arrived outside our home, the walk up the path to the door was not what I imagined. My arms were empty. There was no baby with us. Something that was supposed to be so joyous and full of happiness was not. I cried again as soon as we walked through the front door.

I had a shower so I could get back to the hospital. When we arrived we realised our baby had been placed into another machine with the blue UV light due to jaundice. She still had C-pap equipment for oxygen, and tubes and wires galore. The nurses said she had jaundice but it was common and not to worry. As I had seen jaundice first-hand with my nephews previously I wasn't too alarmed by it and knew it was under control. She also had to be given antibiotics via drip for fluid that doctors had found on her lungs.

I began expressing colostrum so the nurses could tube feed our baby. It was only 0.5-1.0ml but it was liquid gold! It was all new to me. It was extremely difficult to bring in my milk. Emotions were running wild, I was tired, stressed and didn't know what to do when it came to expressing. But I did what I could.

I cried a lot around this time - at least five times a day. I started to feel and think strange. I didn't feel like I had a connection to my child. I wanted to be a normal mother, one who could hold her baby.

But we saw Olivia grow a little bit each day. When she was four days old, I was asked if I wanted to hold her. I watched the nurses open the incubator and hold all the tubes and wires while one of them placed her on my chest. Instant warmth and comfort. I tear up as I write this because it's a feeling that I will never forget. That was the moment I felt the connection. It was an instant love. Before this, I had loved my daughter but there was something missing. As soon as I held her this all changed. I was in love. She was mine and I was hers. I would do anything to protect her.

The days went on and she progressed well. Every three hours I would be there for nappy changes, cleaning her down with a saline solution, tube feeds, cuddles and singing her lullabies. I was on top of the world. Spending time in NICU wasn't the vision I originally had when I was pregnant with her but it would do - as long as I had her.

One day I returned to the hospital and could not find my baby. I frantically searched for her until a nurse asked which baby I was looking for and I said Olivia Panetta. She laughed and said, "It's OK, she has been moved to bay 4." I sighed with relief. Bay 4 was were babies were placed when they were nearly ready to go home. I rushed to bay 4. There she was, patiently waiting with her little eyes open and staring around the room. She was out of her incubator and in a normal crib/bassinet on wheels. She still had wires and tubes attached to her. The doctor came and told me she was doing great and that it was feed and grow from here on in. I was so happy I couldn't wipe the smile off my face.

A couple of days passed and we were trying to latch her, however she just couldn't suck. The nurses told me that babies learn the sucking technique around 36 weeks gestation. She had not reached this stage yet. Tube feeding while she leant up against my breast was the way to encourage her. She tried a little bit but would fall asleep while sucking.

Another day passed, and my husband and I couldn't be happier with how our little girl was growing. I walked into the NICU all smiles, only to have it quickly wiped off my face. The doctors were hovering over my baby. They told me that her heart rate jumped and then dropped. They also heard a heart murmur. This was all new language to me. I didn't know what a heart murmur was. They said they were organising a cardiologist from Westmead Children's Hospital to check her. He would be there later on in the day. I sat by her side and did not move. The day passed and the specialist never showed up.

This is when I met Kate, a nurse I will never forget. She introduced herself and said it was a good sign that he hadn't showed up yet because it meant they didn't believe it was urgent. She reassured me everything was going to be OK. The day ended and I was emotional once again.

The next day I went back into the hospital and sat and waited for the specialist. This time he showed up! He listened to her heart and checked her reports and said absolutely no heart murmur could be heard. He said it might have been an error in the machinery. What a relief!

Then my world came crashing down once again. I walked in one morning and saw my daughter turned on her belly, bottom in the air and a light on her back. No nappy on. I looked closely and saw a hole in the base of her spine, almost where her tailbone is but lower down towards her bottom. It was something I had never seen before. I asked the nurse what had happened and she replied, "I'm so sorry, I cannot discuss this with you. I have to get the doctor." My heart began to race with fear and I felt sick.

The doctor approached me calmly and said, "Hello Mrs Panetta, I have just been told you wanted to speak with me about your daughter." I asked him what the hole was on the base of her spine. He told me it was a sacral dimple and they had ordered an ultrasound to be performed on it. He explained that a sacral dimple was associated with spina bifida. The ultrasound would determine how deep the sacral dimple is and whether she did have spina bifida.

The doctor carried on talking but I couldn't hear a thing. The room was spinning, my heart was racing, and I held back tears. When he stopped speaking, all I could stammer out was, "But she's kicking her legs!" and he agreed that was a good sign. I left the room after the doctor had gone, as I couldn't hold back tears. I called my husband, hysterical. He was at work but I asked him to come quickly as I needed him. I couldn't be there alone.

The day passed and the following day the scan was done. I was shaking as the doctors approached us. They said the scan was clear and confirmed that even though she did indeed have a sacral dimple it was not deep enough for spina bifida. They said she might experience lower back pain in later life but was otherwise a healthy little child. The tears this time were happy ones.

A week went by and then another. Our little girl was growing beautifully. She had a head full of hair and big brown eyes. She looked premature still but she was perfect. However, my milk dried up and I couldn't express at all. I felt like a failure. The nurse who I will cherish forever, Kate, reminded me that as long as Olivia was getting food and growing, I was doing a great job.

Kate suggested we try formula. I was hesitant, but as soon as we gave her the bottle, my daughter latched onto the teat and sucked away. She drank almost the whole bottle and instantly fell asleep. She was satisfied after her big feed. The days went on and we continued with the formula. She grew and grew. We were over the moon!
The NICU began to feel like a second home. We knew all the nurses and some of the other mums. One morning, I came into the hospital as usual and the head registrar came and sat beside me and asked if we were ready to take Olivia home. I said, "I can't wait

until we get to take her home. It's everything I've been waiting for." She then said, "I think she's ready to go home today." My eyes lit up and I couldn't stop grinning. The head registrar said the doctors just had to check Olivia and confirm she was OK to leave and then we would be discharged. I raced home and packed a going home outfit and lots of blankets, as the day was freezing cold.

I arrived back at the hospital and found the doctors in the room. They said she was ready to go home. The nurses all had smiles on their faces and wished us well. The doctors asked us to bring her back in three days so they could check her to make sure she was gaining weight and that all was OK.

Suddenly, a loud scream and wailing broke in to our happiness. I jumped and immediately looked towards the door of our bay. Nurses and doctors surrounded another mother and father, trying to console them and hold them up. They had just lost their baby. My heart broke for them. Even though I was so happy that I was taking my daughter home, I couldn't help but feel terribly sad and angry at the world for taking that little baby away. I still think about that family to this day and remember their screams and crying.

Some people don't realise how lucky they are to have healthy babies, or better yet to be given the chance to carry a baby without any difficulty. There are families out there who would long to have a baby but can't.

During our NICU experience, we saw newborn babies being brought out of addictions to ice and other drugs that their mothers took while pregnant. There was another child who was alone day in and day out - his mum left and never returned for him. Another child who had a mother that used to come once a week wearing green prison wear. And a decent, loving family that lost their baby. These memories will stick with us forever. We are grateful for everything that Nepean NICU did for us. They will forever be a part of our family.

Natalie Panetta

Our Journey to Happiness

I was just 19 years old in 1999 when I married Kevin, and the furthest thing from my mind was not being able to get pregnant. Our goal was a honeymoon baby – it never occurred to us that it wouldn't happen. Our honeymoon lasted for six weeks; we had all the time in the world. I had never been on the pill, we were both young and healthy and wasn't this what I'd always planned?

When we arrived back home, I was not pregnant. Two periods had been and gone since being married and I was thinking, wow, how can I not be pregnant?

We tried for one whole year and by this time I was getting quite concerned that I was not falling pregnant. So I went to my GP, who told me I was young, don't stress, and keep trying. Well, that didn't sit well with Kevin and me, as we really wanted to start a family.

Over the next few months I did lots of research and asked other ladies what they did when they had trouble getting pregnant. A lot of women had used an ovulation tester, so I started to check my temperature and doing the whole wee-on-the-stick thing to find out when I was ovulating. Throughout the months I tried this but my hormone levels stayed the same. I began to really fear that getting pregnant was not going to be possible for me, so I headed straight back to the doctors.

This time I was taken seriously and referred to a gynecologist, Dr Lovell. But it took nine weeks to get an appointment with Dr Lovell, a process which left me feeling upset and confused. Eventually we got to see Dr Lovell. She was sweet, and talked softly but firmly. She told me, "We need to do further testing on both you and your husband so we can sort this out."

We left that office with a stack of paperwork. The lovely receptionist booked us for another appointment in three weeks.

The next few weeks were busy. At that time I owned a hair and beauty salon, and we were in peak season. I loved my job, loved managing my business and my staff. But behind that was this immense weight of worry about our results. I had blood tests and scans booked, and Kevin had to do a series of sperm count tests.

When we went back to the doctor's, it was hard to sit in the waiting room surrounded by pregnant women. I just wanted to scream! Dr Lovell did not have good news for us. I had polycystic ovaries and a blockage in my left tube and my left ovary had cysts all over it. She then said, "I am really sorry to tell you but Kevin has a low sperm count." It felt like a bullet just went through my heart. Kevin said to me, "I am sorry, honey." But I replied, "Don't be sorry - it's you and me."

I don't remember much else of what Dr Lovell said, but she did advise us to look into IVF. The next few weeks were hard, and I cried a lot. I kept asking, why me? Kevin was amazing support. He would lie with me and let me cry, and he would always know the right things to say.

We had to wait three months for our appointment at IVF Australia. It felt like all we did was wait and worry. During this time I turned 21 and it felt like time was ticking. All around me friends and family were getting pregnant. Each time I heard the news my heart would break a little more but the words that followed would be, "Congrats, that's great news." As we had kept our pregnancy struggles to ourselves, keeping a straight face was getting harder and harder.

Yippee!! The day for our IVF appointment arrived and I was more excited than Christmas. We arrived at the clinic and again we were bombarded with paperwork - the questions were so in-depth and personal. The walls of the clinic were covered in people's success stories and beautiful baby photos. I sat there and read some of them and, for the first time since this journey began, hope started to creep in.

Dr Joel Bernstein talked to us about the process and as I had problems and Kevin had problems the type of IVF process required for us would be the latest technique called ICSI. The process involved the collection of my eggs and the collection of Kevin's sperm. The sperm was inserted directly in the egg so that the hardest job was done and all that needed to happen is the fertilisation process. The doctor then proceeded to fill out our paperwork so we could start the cycle. Our bloods were taken by the nurse and we were given a chart to follow and an instruction book. Our nurse was wonderful; so understanding and calm.

We left with an overload of information and the instructions to "live by your phone" as the nurse would call us about our results. The nurse called to tell us that we needed to let the clinic know when my period starts. More waiting – by now I love waiting! Day one of my period arrived and the nurse told me I needed to come in for blood tests starting on day five of my period. For seven days in a row I had blood taken and on the seventh day the nurse told me that things were looking positive. She handed me a bag containing my hormone injections, pessaries and other tablets. She outlined how to use them and guided me though the upcoming procedure.

Every day for six weeks, at 6pm, I self-administered the hormone treatment. Our lives now revolved around hormone injections and doctor's appointments. I became so focused on this treatment. I put all my energy, prayers and emotion into trying to stay confident and positive each day.

The injections made me bloat up and my tummy was so sore and bruised. But finally we were given some good news. The nurse said, "Your eggs are looking good, nice and full, and lots of follicles there." I was booked in to day surgery for egg collection. We talked that night about the next chapter in our lives and the thought of finally getting pregnant, and I was so excited

On egg collection day I was so nervous; but Kevin reassured me and kept me confident. While I had my eggs harvested, Kevin was in the next room collecting sperm so the cross match can be done. When I woke up I was told 12 eggs had been collected. The scientist, Renee, came out to tell us that the cross matching had been done. So now we had to go home and wait for the results. It was a funny mixture of feelings - happy, sad, worried, relieved, concerned and most of all excited that in a few days those embryos would be implanted.

The next day Renee phoned to tell us that of the 12 only six had continued to split and divide; so only six viable embryos. That was a hard blow. All those injections, a day surgery, all the discomfort - and I only had six left. The tears started flowing again, and I couldn't believe this was happening. Renee called the next day to tell us we needed to come into the clinic for an embryo transfer. The rest of the viable embryos would be frozen.

On transfer day we were taken into a very cold, very sterile room to wait. Finally the embryo transfer was done. We were told to carry on as normal, but to come back in 14 days. If my period arrived I was to call the clinic asap. What on earth is 'normal' when you are continually racing to the bathroom to check if you have any spotting and every little pain or twitch makes you worry? It got so tense that every time I called Kevin his first words would be, "Is everything OK?"

We made it to day 14. We arrived at the clinic at 6.30am to be first in line to have bloods. We went straight though and I was getting a little excited. But we were faced with a fresh slap in the face when, two hours after leaving the clinic, my period arrived. I looked down at my underwear in shock! I had made it to 14 days and was beginning to hope. What a cruel surprise. I could hear in Kevin's voice how disappointed he was but he replied, "It's OK honey. It was the first try - we will go again."
I spent the whole morning in bed crying and feeling so let down. I wondered, how did it not take - it was fertilized and it was in there?

A phone call from the clinic confirmed what I already knew – I wasn't pregnant. I then started thinking that maybe it's me; maybe I am not cut out to be pregnant, and maybe it's my body's way of telling me, don't go there. Kevin arrived home and he was so supportive. Not once did he say "don't worry" or "get over it". Not once did he let me feel I was letting him down. Five more times over a 14-month period we went through the process, and every time was a failure. By now Kevin and I were drained physically, emotionally and financially. My dream of having my own baby was slipping away. There were babies being born all around me and everywhere I looked were pregnant ladies. And then there was me, feeling angrier by the day.

By this time all my embryos were used up so the process for another egg collection began with another round of hormone injections and blood tests and the long drive down to the clinic., as well as running my successful business and keeping my personal life locked up so the world thought I was normal.

The time arrived for my next egg collection but this time I hypostemulated, which meant my body went into overdrive and the follicles had over-produced so they had to give me a drug to reverse it. So no eggs collected that day. Yet another effort that was all for nothing.

The next egg collection was successful and I got 22 eggs – wow! The doctor and scientist were really happy, and I was feeling well after this egg collection. I was referred to another specialist, Dr David Knight, who was studying and trying new techniques that I might benefit from. We met with Dr Knight and immediately I felt I was in good hands. We returned to the clinic three days later for a fresh transfer. Hopes were high. The doctor was confident and we were too.
During the transfer, the doctor noticed my uterus was tilted and that was why we were having so much trouble. He placed the embryo in a higher spot and said, "Let's give that a go."

Six days later my period arrived. I sobbed to my mum; "I am not doing this anymore. You wouldn't do this to a dog - I am done." My mum was so strong and brave. She said, "You can do it and I will hold your hand the whole way." I agreed to go one more time; after that I could say I did all I could. My mum came each day during that round to my blood tests and spoke with the doctor and nurses and kept my chin up. It was a relief for Kevin because I know he was tired from trying to keep me strong and he was hurting just as much as me.

The last round began in October 2003, a Monday morning and a public holiday. The staff were amazing, working any time that my body's hormones were ready. We entered the transfer room and everything was ready to go. The doctor gave me a booster to place under my bottom to boost me up and back at the right angle. On this transfer we decided to have two embryos implanted. The transfer went smooth, and it was less painful and less invasive. The doctor said, "Fingers crossed, and enjoy the rest of your day off."
I took this transfer with a very carefree attitude. I had already decided that the transfer was not going to work and that I was just going through the motions to say that I had tried my best. The next 14 days were spent working long hours, taking my medication and living life.

Day 14 arrived – again - and mum and me went back to the clinic for the dreaded blood test. After a short wait Anne, the nurse, took me through. Anne's smile was always so comforting and warm. As she took my blood she talked to me about staying positive and happy and enjoying the journey. I always put on a strong face but inside I was a mess. The bloods were done and Anne said she would call me at 11am.

The car ride home was quiet. I think my mum had everything crossed and I believe that she had never prayed so much. But she always spoke so confident and calmly, and always said the right things.

We arrived home and my mum stayed with me. We kept ourselves busy around the house - making beds and hanging washing - and at exactly 11am the home phone rang. It was Anne from the clinic. I put the phone on loudspeaker so Mum could hear, as I was not repeating any bad news. "Congratulations, you're pregnant," Anne said. I was silent for a while then responded with, "Are you sure?" She said, "Yes your levels are very high and to keep an eye on things we need you to come down tomorrow morning for more bloods." I managed to stammer out a "thank you" and hung up.

Well, the tears rolled again but this time they were tears of joy. My mum was excited and crying too. I then called Kevin and before he could say hello I blurt out, "It bloody worked, we are having a baby!" He too was very emotional and happy and relieved. Next I called my dad. After we'd said our hellos, he asked me why I was calling. I said, "Because you're going to be a Nunnu (Grandfather) again." There was silence on the other end. "Dad? Dad are you OK?" He said, "Yes, I am just so happy. Thank god." I could hear the happiness in his voice. Kevin called his mum and she too was overjoyed.

The next day arrived and I had never been so eager to get to the clinic. My bloods were taken and an ultrasound was done. The doctor had some more news for us: we were expecting twins! For the first time in a long time I smiled, and it was a real smile.

At my next appointment a week later, Anne told me I was ready to see a gynecologist. "Are you sure?" I asked. She said, "I am more than sure, you are nearly six weeks pregnant and our job is done." As much as I had dreaded going to the clinic, it had become a safe place. But I called the gynecologist and made an appointment to see her when I reach eight weeks pregnant.

By week seven I was vomiting all day, every day - but I didn't care. My days consisted of working and vomiting. Eventually the vomiting got so bad I was admitted to hospital. My gyno, Dr Lovell, met me at the hospital in the maternity ward, and checked me over. She put me straight onto an IV drip and ordered an ultrasound. I felt afraid again - nine months is such a long time when you have no control over what's happening. The ultrasound was done and during the scan Dr Lovell told me that Twin A was not doing as well as Twin B and she was a little concerned. She kept me in for five days and during that time I was still vomiting but not as bad.

At this time, Kevin and I decided to sell the business and focus on this pregnancy. The shop sold in four weeks and I spent my time resting at home, still vomiting. I got up one morning and started doing some washing, when all of a sudden I got cramps. Scared out of my skin I called my mum as Kevin was too far away. Mum said she was on her way and told me to go lie down and don't move. As I lay down I felt wet and realised I was bleeding. As soon as Mum arrived she raced to call Dr Lovell.

Mum took me back to hospital. I was stressing like no tomorrow. But Dr Lovell greeted me calmly. She explained that I had a small tear and that the bleeding should slow down. I went straight down to ultrasound and there it was: two strong heart beats. What an awesome sight. I remained in hospital for seven more days and given more IV fluids and full bed rest. At this stage I was only 11 weeks.

Weeks 11 – 16 were OK. I was still vomiting, and the only thing I could eat were pizza and Pepsi, and very little of that. I visited Dr Lovell at her clinic each Wednesday at 12.30 and she was happy with my progress. Each week she did a small ultrasound and twin A was always smaller than twin B. Twin A was sitting very low and Twin B was sitting higher.

Week 17 was a sad week. One morning I woke to heavy bleeding. Kevin took me straight to the hospital. Dr Lovell examined me and did an ultrasound. She said, "Twin A is coming away - I am sorry, but this baby is not going to make it, how ever Twin B is happy as, so that's very important." Dr Lovell explained that I would have heavy bleeding but I might not pass the baby as it could be absorbed and would pass through during labour. I bled for the remaining time of my pregnancy. I was so sad, and I worried for my baby I was still carrying. I worried about my baby I lost and never met. I had so many emotions.

I left hospital and continued my pregnancy journey. The weeks passed quickly and before we knew it I was 35 weeks pregnant. My beautiful family gave me a surprise baby shower at my sister-in-law's house. Kevin had a hard time convincing me to get in the car. I kept saying, "I don't want to go visiting." He said, "You stay home all day, every day and the only outing you have is to doctor's appointments!" I'm glad I listened to him because I had the best time and I am forever grateful to my family for that experience.

At 39 weeks pregnant Dr Lovell said to me, "I don't think I will be seeing you in my clinic for a check-up again - I think I will be seeing you in the labour ward." I was filled with excitement each day, wondering if today was the day.

My waters broke one Sunday morning in June. I felt so happy. I yelled out to Kevin, "Get up, get up! It's happening - my waters just broke!" I called my mum to tell her the news and ask her to meet us at the hospital.

By now I was a regular at the maternity ward so all the nurses were excited for me. I just couldn't wait to meet my baby. We still didn't know if we would be welcoming a boy or a girl. When we had the transfer done I knew we had one girl and one boy embryo put in and through the whole process and all the ultrasounds we never found out. It didn't matter to me. I was having a baby – woo-hoo!

I laboured for 24 long hours, and I had every pain relief offered to me. Kevin and Mum were there the whole time, as was Dr Lovell. After 17 hours an epidural was ordered for me as I had stopped dilating. After receiving the epidural my body relaxed and I started dilating again.

At exactly 6am on 21 June I felt the need to push so I did. I heard my mum say, "It's a boy! You did it, you did it!" It was such an emotional moment. The look of relief and joy on Mum's face will stay with me forever. Kevin cried, he was so happy it was a boy and so happy we had a child; a child of our own.

We named him Lewis John Buhagiar, after Kevin's deceased dad. He was born at 6.05am on 21 June 2004, weighing 8 pound 4 ounces and 50 cm tall. It's the shortest day of the year in Australia, but the happiest for us. We called our family and friends and everyone was excited by the news.

Kevin and my mum stood by me during the whole five-year process of trying to have this baby. But as joy filled my heart I still felt sadness for my daughter who never made the journey. I thought about what she would have looked like. Her name would have been Victoria Grace after my mum and my grandmother. I still think about her every day.

I tried IVF seven more times over the next eight years until the time came that we decided we'd had enough. We have Lewis and we are more than grateful. Lewis is a kind and softhearted kid who will be turning 12 this year.

Writing this story has helped me understand the importance of life and the heartache that goes into being a parent. The journey was a long rough ride but we got through it. We had support from our family and friends, and most of all we had each other.

I never judge people on how many kids they have or don't have, as every family has their own story.

So many people helped me on this journey. I wish to thank my husband Kevin, my mum, IVF Australia, Dr Lovell, all the nurses at Nepean Private Hospital, my clinic nurse Anne, Dr David Knight, Dr Joel Bernstein and our scientist Renee.

                Jeanette Buhagiar - Sydney Australia

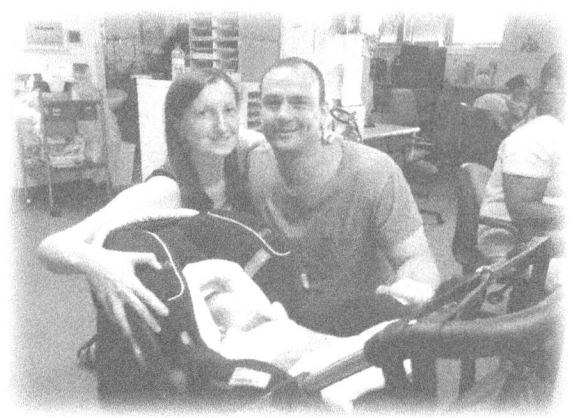

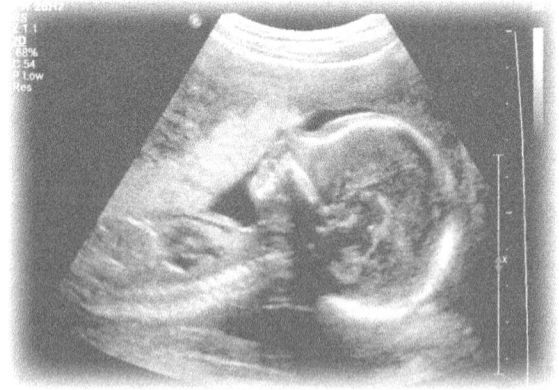

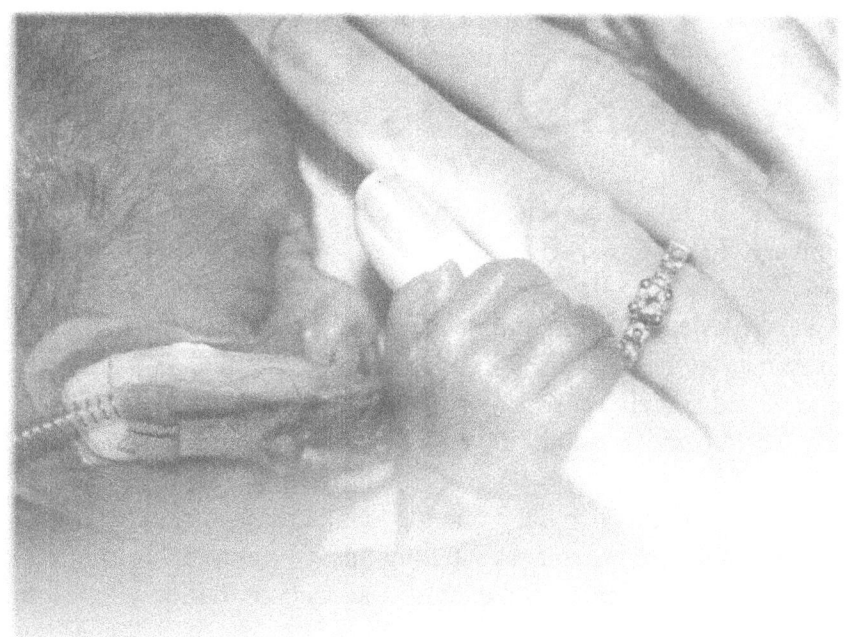

Our Precious Boys

When you hold your first born in your arms time stands still. You exist in a love bubble. You're overwhelmed at the thought of this precious child making you a mother. Making you parents.
I'm a mother, went through my head many times as I gave birth to my son.

I couldn't wait to see him, hold him and see who he looked like.
I took in every part of my beautiful little bundle. Ten fingers, 10 tiny toes, little button nose, his smell, the curve of his lips, the softness of his skin and downy hair.
I will never forget that moment with my first born, my little Charlie Jacob.

Perfect and small. My hands, his daddy's lips, dark hair, a sweet smell, his beauty. Perfect in every way.
These memories will last a lifetime and be etched in my mind forever. My lasting memory of a little boy I would never take home.

Charlie was born at 19 weeks and one day, weighing just 256 grams. He was born breathing, and lived for 30 minutes before he grew his angel wings.

A pre-term loss due to 'cervical incompetence'.
I will never forget that day. It was the hottest day in 60 years: 8 January, 2013.

I was experiencing pain, but had no idea I was in labour. I was examined and told I was 3cm dilated, and sadly, that I was in labour and would be delivering my son with no chance of survival.
My world came crashing down.

Why us? Why this baby, the one we longed for and tried for seven years - with numerous IVF treatments, two early miscarriages, failed cycles, and cancelled cycles - to conceive. It didn't seem real. It was so unfair.

My IVF journey was an emotional rollercoaster I thought was over once I had finally conceived. I was relieved of the challenge of emotions I experienced for so long; the heartbreak and disappointment seemed to be over once I heard a healthy heartbeat at our eight-week scan.

I felt like I'd boarded the rollercoaster again, and was free falling. Charlie arrived late in the afternoon on that day. He was perfect. I was in awe of how beautiful he was. He was perfectly formed, just incredibly small.

We had some time with him and then farewelled our little boy. Handing him to our midwife Nicolle, who I will never forget. She was so supportive. I will always be grateful to her. I saw her tears and heartbreak too.

Those brief moments with Charlie were wrenching, but special too, as with any birth; a moment in time etched in your mind forever.
I sat in the garden at the hospital the night that Charlie was born in a state of disbelief.

I placed my hands on my belly, realising my hopes and dreams for him were gone. He was so wanted and he was gone.
I was devastated but also incredibly proud. I felt very blessed despite the circumstances. I had become a mother that day to a precious little boy.

He's not here, but I'm still his mother and he's my son. My first born; my precious Angel.

The weeks that followed his loss were incredibly hard. Having to make arrangements for his final resting place, his cremation, our personal memorial service - all so hard and heartbreaking. A place we can visit and special songs are all that is left to remember him. The love I held for Charlie helped me put one foot in front of the other in a personal journey that helped me learn so much about myself. There were things I didn't know about myself in my 39 years of life.

I was much stronger than I realised and more resilient than I ever thought possible.
I walked with a different beat. I stopped rushing around and took time in everything I did. I used my senses to take in the beauty of my surroundings. I slowed right down and took better care of myself. I had always put everyone ahead of myself, but now it was important to take a bit of that selflessness for myself.
We decided to give IVF another go a short few months after losing Charlie. Walking back into the clinic was difficult. I never saw myself going back, except to show off the pride and joy they helped us bring into the world.

We were met with open arms and supported through the next chapter of our IVF journey.
We were incredibly blessed to fall pregnant with a fresh transfer following egg collection. I was so relieved. Part of my fear in receiving more treatment was another long road, like we had had with Charlie, to fall pregnant again.

I had a nervous pregnancy, often consumed with fear. Every twinge, pain or discomfort made me more anxious.

The day of my eight-week scan I bled. A subchorionic hemotoma was the cause. I continued to bleed heavily through to 16 weeks, when I was given a cervical stitch. I found it hard to connect with my growing baby, not knowing what would come of the constant bleeding I was experiencing.

But each scan showed a strong, healthy baby. And we were given the all-clear at our anomaly scan at 18 weeks. Our baby was OK. Our baby - another son - was happy and healthy, and I could finally relax.

I ticked the weeks off in my mind. Oh, the relief when I made it past 19 weeks. With each week that passed I became more relaxed and eased into my pregnancy.

At 24 weeks I started experiencing pain. I was told it was likely to be Braxton Hicks. I went to the hospital to be checked out and was reassured there was nothing to worry about. Two days passed and I was still experiencing discomfort. After an examination and monitoring I was told I was having contractions.

I was admitted to hospital and given the necessary medication to ease my contractions, as well as steroids and, in the days that followed, a magnesium infusion. My pregnancy would be seen out in hospital on bed rest.

I was seen by NICU doctors and given statistics in hope of reassuring me. A horrible thing to have worrying at your mind; a conversation no mother wants to have. As the days passed the survival rates went up and my worry eased, a little.

At 26 weeks five days, I started bleeding. I was rushed to another hospital, out of our local area, as there were no longer NICU beds at our admitting hospital. I got the last bed in NSW.

Our little Hunter Charlie arrived, weighing 908 grams, on 15 October, 2013. He was born at 27 weeks and one day. It was a very bittersweet day for me. This day is pregnancy and infant loss remembrance day - a day on which I would remember my little Charlie taken too soon, and celebrate the birth of my newborn son.

Our first meeting was an emotional one. I was excited to finally meet our little Hunter, but feared I would lose him too. He was so tiny. Tubes and the noise of monitors and machinery surrounded him. I was frightened.

He was such a beautiful little boy, a blessing, our miracle. So much like his brother. Just like his dad.

Hunter battled any odds and all the possible outcomes I was told of. He was on CPAP for three days and then breathing on his own. We were told he would, once strong enough in a few weeks, be transferred to a hospital closer to home. To our surprise Hunter was transferred after just nine days from intensive care to a high dependency ward at another hospital. He was a fighter. He was determined to stay. My many prayers had been answered.

The NICU journey isn't easy. We were fortunate that Hunter had no major medical complications and grew as he was expected. The hardest thing was leaving at the end of every day, and grieving for the moments you want as a mother, at home with your baby. Instead of waking to a hungry baby I was expressing every three hours and cried most nights, just wanting him home with us, in the comfort of our home. NICU was the home away from home for 10 weeks.

We were discharged on Christmas Eve of 2013. What a perfect Christmas gift!

We settled into life as parents beautifully. Hunter was an easy baby, calm and settled. He was such a blessing; a true little miracle.

There were so many times, looking into Hunter's eyes, I would think of Charlie and miss him even more, knowing I missed the same precious moments with him.

I would be consumed with grief at times. I wished he was with us and our boys could be together.

Looking back, I wish I had accessed the support services offered to me. At the time I felt well-supported from family and friends.

I didn't want to become too emotional during my pregnancy with Hunter, fearing my emotions would affect the outcome of my pregnancy.

Nothing can prepare you for the emotions that come flooding back when your next child enters the world following a loss. For me, it wasn't only grief due to my loss but grief over many things. I didn't get to experience what it was like to be pregnant to term, the swollen ankles, the stretch marks a reminder of the children I carried, holding my baby after birth, snapping our first family photo in the delivery room with tears of joy in our eyes, breastfeeding from day one, newborn professional photos...The list goes on.

I felt no-one really understood what I went through. The IVF, my loss and then the NICU journey. There was no-one I could talk to, other than my partner, who truly understood. He walked this road with me and he hurt too.

I would talk about my loss and would be met with silence or words and comments that hurt.

As grieving mothers, all we want is to be heard and be listened to when we find the courage to talk. To hear words of comfort, for our loss and our babies' short lives. To have the journey to become a mother and a father validated. To speak of the baby that isn't here, but is still part of our family. To always remember and never forget.

I will always be grateful to partner Jason, my loving family, dearest friends, the midwives of Royal North Shore, especially Nicolle, the incredible staff at Westmead fertility clinic, Nepean and Royal North Shore Neonatal Intensive Care Unit doctors, nurses and support staff.

2013 was an intense year. It commenced with heartache with the loss of Charlie, but ended in such joy. Our Hunter - our little miracle, our ray of sunshine, our precious rainbow baby - was home. We were finally a family. A family with two boys; one who watches over us and the other a reminder of how precious life really is..

Meredith Bale - Sydney, Australia

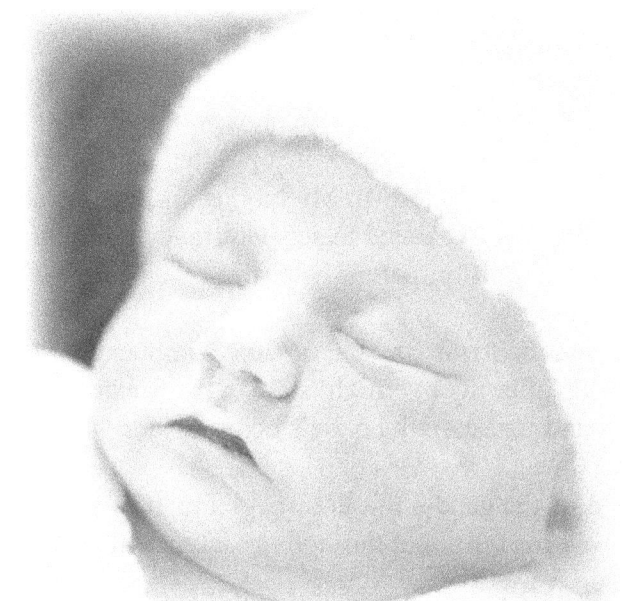

Our Precious Gem - Ruby
22-11-14

All week I hadn't been feeling well. All I could think was, "God, it can't be that long until Iabour and this baby comes out."
I was admitted to our little local hospital on 16 November, 2014, with a high heart rate and feeling "blah". I was booked in for my routine scan the next day. That night, I got no sleep, I was hungry, I ate, I threw up and then the fire alarm went off - someone was having a hot shower and the steam set the alarm off. The next morning I couldn't wait to get out of there, although the staff were nice and all. But who wants to stay in hospital?

That Monday morning after my drip was taken out and I was getting ready to be released, I asked the nurse if what they had given me to try and stop the nausea and vomiting, could possibly have had an adverse reaction and be the cause of me feeling bruised all over. Unknown to anyone, this was my body starting to shut down.

Kyle, my husband, had to work that day, as he had not long started his dream job. So Mum - ah, thank god for my mum! - She came with me to my scan which was 45 minutes away. The baby was fine, all well, although he or she (we chose not to find out the sex) hadn't put on much weight but we just put that down to me not being able to keep anything down. My mother-in-law was also present at the scan. She was so excited to see her grandchild moving around on the screen and most importantly, hearing the heartbeat.

I had an appointment with my GP on 20 November, 2014. This was just a check-up after my overnight stay on the Sunday. He got the Doppler out and we heard the baby's heartbeat for what was to be the very last time.
We didn't know the gender of our sweet baby. It was going to be a surprise, a way for me to get through my labour - that was my train of thought, anyway.

On 21 November, 2014, I was sick, sick, sick. I thought that this might be the day. I couldn't keep anything down, not even water. I felt like absolute crap, I would lie down and not be able to get comfortable and would throw up again and again, time after time. I didn't have any specific pain but I ached all over. I just thought that this was me and how I am when I'm pregnant.

Kyle came home at lunch time; he was passing through town and decided he would check on me. I can remember he told me I looked like crap. Mum also called in and said the same.

At about 10.30pm, I rang Mum and told her that I just didn't feel right. I had been telling this to Kyle but he was so exhausted from his new job, he just wanted to go to bed and sleep. I can still hear Mum's voice, "Well, I suggest if you don't feel right, you go to hospital, or at least, ring the maternity ward. You have their number, don't you?" I agreed with her and rang the maternity ward at the hospital where I was going to give birth.

I wish I could remember the lady's name, she was lovely (insert sarcasm). I told her of my concerns to which she replied, "Sounds like you're just not handling the pain that goes with labour." Okie dokie then! I asked her if I should come in, she said I could if I wanted to. I then said, "OK, well, we will be there in about an hour."

I then went and broke the news to my husband, and he wasn't all that impressed. I grabbed the baby's hospital bag and Kyle grabbed mine and his. I rang Mum to let her know that we were heading to the hospital.

On the way, we discussed and finalised boy's and girl's names. We laughed about the fact that we were driving the ute, which hadn't yet had the baby capsule installed. We were so excited that this could be it, this could be the beginning of us being parents.

We arrived at the hospital around 11.15pm. It was dark and pretty quiet for a Friday night. We were taken up to the maternity ward - well, actually, we were given directions on how to get there. I explained again to a group of midwives what had been happening.

The first thing they did was lay me down and check my blood pressure, which was fine. They did a urine test, also fine. Then it was time to be put on the heart beat machine. We were still pretty excited. The midwife spent a couple of minutes moving the belly bands around, trying to find the baby's heartbeat. She said she had found it but was going to get one of the gynecologists to come in and have a good listen. We still weren't worried. It didn't even occur to us that anything horrible could go wrong.

The gynecologist came in with a portable ultrasound machine. He tried to find the heart beat but couldn't. He told us that someone must have been fiddling with the dials on the laptop, so he went to find the other machine. He still couldn't find our baby's heartbeat. After this, I can't remember much, although I do recall being told that they were going to call the "head honcho" in as he would be the best bet at finding the heartbeat. Kyle held my hand.

Suddenly we were hearing the most stupid, ridiculous, unthinkable sentence any parents could ever hear: "I'm sorry, I can't find the

heartbeat, there is no heartbeat, I am so very sorry." These words shouldn't even exist.
I said in a very stern voice, "Excuse me? What? You have to be joking!"

Kyle just fell to the floor and started crying. My heart broke. Actually, it shattered into a million bloody freaking pieces.
After a moment - or maybe a million - I asked what was going to happen now. After another scan to confirm our precious baby had no heartbeat, we were told to think about a few things, including whether to be induced or go home and wait? Pain relief? Calling family?

We decided to be induced. I wanted to meet our baby. And I wanted pain relief; if my baby was going to be stillborn, I wasn't going to go through the physical pain if I could help it.

We were taken to a lovely room away from all the crying babies. This is where we made the phone calls. Kyle called his parents and I called mine. We cried. We cried a lot. My parents came straight to the hospital. I will never be able to erase the looks on Mum's and Dad's faces as they walked through the door.

Kyle slept, he must have been buggered. Mum rubbed my back and Dad sat in a chair, devastated. Mum, Dad and Kyle were there the whole time, for which I will never be able to thank them enough.
I had my first lot of induction gel at around 3.30am. It was gross. And this is about all I actually remember.

Our midwife, Lauren, was doing my observations and getting ready for my second lot of gel when my heart-rate plummeted and my blood pressure went through the roof. She had to call for help.
I do remember walking, because I wasn't going anywhere in a wheelchair, down the hall with my hospital gown wide open, to the room where they were going to prepare me for an emergency c-section. Three nurses had trouble putting the catheter in, I had only produced about 3ml of urine over a long period of time, and my kidneys had shut down. Bloods also showed that my liver function

was on its way out too. I was now in multi organ failure. It must have been scary, scary stuff for Kyle, Mum and Dad. They had just lost a child and grandchild and were now facing the possibility of losing a wife and daughter.

The medical team had great difficulty in finding my veins. I was so swollen, and I later found out I was 33kgs heavier – because of excess fluid - than I was at my last appointment on the Monday before.
I can remember putting on the hair net and laughing about my 'sexy' stockings.

Lauren, our beautiful midwife, was with me the whole way. She asked us what we wanted to happen with the baby once he or she was born. Did we want baby to stay with me the whole time or did we want him or her to go to the morgue? I wanted bubs to stay with me, even though I was going to be under a general anesthetic. Lauren kept this promise. She also took my phone into theatre so she could take photos of our precious angel as soon as he or she was born.

On Saturday, 22 November, 2014 at 11:33am Ruby Gwen Margaret Williams was born sleeping. She weighed 6lbs 10ozs at 36 weeks and six days gestation. It was predicted she would have been around the 10 pound mark if I had gone full term.

It wasn't until around 2.15pm that we got out of theatre and up to ICU and Kyle could see me and meet our brand new, sleeping, but so beautiful baby girl. Our Ruby girl.

As I was still waking up, Kyle introduced our daughter to everyone. Although we were both devastated, we were as proud as punch. It was like we put the fact that she was born sleeping aside for a second. We wanted to show our baby girl off to the whole world!
Our parents were the first ones to meet Ruby, followed by our brothers and sisters and our closest friends which are family anyway. We broke the record of visitors in an ICU room at once for the hospital. Twenty-two people, all there for us and our daughter.

When I finally came to, I can remember Kyle handing Ruby to me and saying, "We had a baby girl, Ruby, and she's beautiful. Would you like to hold her?" Of course I did. We both spent some time checking her out, over and over again. We were in total awe of what the two of us had made, all by ourselves. She was, and still is, perfect.

Kyle slept up in ICU with us, his girls, for two nights before we were moved to the maternity ward.

While still in ICU, we got to bathe Ruby, dress her, kiss her, cuddle her, one of our dearest friends read her a book, loads of photos were taken (I'm so happy everyone went snap happy). Impressionable Kids came in and did Ruby's hand and feet impressions. We cut a lock of her hair, her fuzzy wuzzy hair.
I can remember undressing her and having skin to skin time with her after Mum had given her a bath, and this was a beautiful time. I remember just rubbing her back and patting her little bottom. I knew she was gone and wasn't coming back, but it's just what came naturally and what I wanted to do.

It didn't seem too long before we were asked if we wanted an autopsy performed on Ruby. This meant that she would have to go to Melbourne and then she would be taken straight to the funeral directors until her funeral. We decided that we needed to send her on a road trip to Melbourne to have it done, for our peace of mind and for our future babies.

Ruby was with us in a cold cot, angel crib, cuddle cot, for two and a half days before she went to Melbourne.
Again, I can only remember bits and pieces. I think it was my body and mind's way of protecting me. I was still fairly doped up and dopey on that Monday we said goodbye. I kissed our daughter goodbye and told her that I loved her so much and then handed her over to Kyle so Lauren, our midwife, could take her to the funeral director. It was so quiet after Ruby left.

The next few days, everyone concentrated on getting me better and healthy again. The doctors said that if I had left it until the Saturday to get checked out, I probably wouldn't be here either. They would have been digging two graves.

It wasn't until the following Friday that things - Ruby - actually hit me. I was well enough for a big ugly dose of stupid reality to hit me fair and square in my heart. This was the beginning of me grieving the loss of my daughter. I cried all night, looked at my phone all night and listened to the baby across the hall cry, all night. The nurses on that night were awesome. One in particular sat with me until I fell asleep in the early hours of the morning, she really was wonderful. The next day I asked if Kyle could stay that night, I needed him to be there with me. They said that it was not a problem at all. I was so relieved.

Not much sleep was got that night. We planned Ruby's whole funeral down to a tee. And we cried a lot, together. We looked at her photos and spoke to her as if she was still here on this earth with us. That night, although it sounds a little weird, was one of the most beautiful nights of my life, and a very important one.

Nine days after giving birth to our angel, I was released from hospital. I still had a lot of physical healing to do as my wound re-opened after having the stitch taken out, so I had a vacuum dressing put on. Our families, oh my god, our families were absolutely beautiful, amazing and supportive, and still are. I can remember Dad telling us not to worry about the funeral costs, whatever we wanted for our girl, we would get. That was such a relief.

The next couple of days were spent confirming the finer details of Ruby's funeral. Also, getting used to people looking at us differently and crossing the road just in front of us to avoid us. One of the biggest changes for me was the smell of our house. I hated it and it took me some time before I could love our house and our home again.

Our beautiful first-born baby girl, Ruby, was buried on 5 December, 2014. Her grave is right in front of my dearest Nan. We wanted them to be as close together as they could get. The day was beautiful, and everything happened just how we planned it.
My sister and Kyle's sister delivered Ruby's short but interesting eulogy and our awesome friend read out a lovely poem. Both our fathers had one of the toughest jobs that day - they carried their granddaughter to her resting place.

Her flowers were bright and colourful and covered the top of her tiny casket. Caskets that size should never have to be made!
The best thing our friend said to us that day while she was hugging us was that we were to stay there for as long as we needed to, no one could tell us that it was time to go. I thank her so much for telling us that.

During my stay in hospital, our families were amazing. If Kyle wasn't with me, my mum was. My dear old Pop, he came and had tea with me every single night, such a pillar of support. Our friends were, and still are, amazing. They speak Ruby's name and talk about her as if she were here with us. They aren't afraid that they might upset us. We love them so much more for this.

So, now our little Miss Ruby is a year old. Her first birthday was a great day, we didn't want it to be sad, and we wanted to celebrate just as any other parents would with a living child. Our family and friends and our midwife all gathered for an early tea at Ruby's place (the cemetery) and of course, a big pink birthday cake. She got presents and cards and we sang happy birthday.

Ruby is also now a big sister. Miss Matilda Mary Lauren was born on 5 February, 2016. She is a spitting image of her big sister and we have no doubt that they have some sort of connection. Matilda and any other future siblings will grow up to know their big sister and how she has changed and made so many lives better. She has definitely done her job down here on earth.

If I could offer one bit of advice or guidance for those who are going through something similar I would say do what you have to do, how you want to do it and when it feels right for you to do it. No one else but you! And be gentle with yourself. Cry when you feel the need to and don't feel one ounce of guilt if you find yourself smiling. You're allowed to!

Annaleise and Kyle Williams - Northern Victoria, Australia

"I felt ready to smother with love another little one, and from the moment we knew I was pregnant I had a feeling it was another boy. I even named him Oliver"

Oliver

I am mum to four children: three living, one not.
I have a 15-year-old daughter from my first marriage and the three from my second marriage. All three from my second marriage were IVF miracle babies.

My first IVF pregnancy was amazing. My husband and I were at the time both defence force members, and as life throws you curveballs, we found I was going in for my first egg collection after he was being deployed to Afghanistan. So while everything was happening with me, he was busy depositing lots of sperm to be frozen. It was quite funny, looking back now.

So off he went, and in I came to have my transfer. We had success on the second attempt, and plenty of eggs on ice too, which was great to know.

Our little man arrived by inducement on Christmas Eve, 2009. His dad had arrived back in the country when I was seven months' pregnant, which was hard to explain to those not in the know! So even though I had now had two pregnancies, I also discovered I had a blood condition that caused me to clot. Not thinking this would impact on my ability to successfully deliver my baby, my IVF specialists had monitored my delivery to a tee. I was in good hands, as was baby boy.

After six months we thought we should start trying again, as age was against me and I did not want to leave our run too late. Another round of transfers, this time more difficult, but then success again! I was amazed at how my body could do this again. I felt ready to smother with love another little one, and from the moment we knew I was pregnant I had a feeling it was another boy. I even named him Oliver - although I never told anyone, including my husband.

Oliver was with me for just under eight weeks, nearly two months. We found out later it was my blood condition that had taken him from us, which was sad in a sense that maybe things could have been different. I had the curette on my birthday, seven days later. That gets me every year, as does the memory of the IVF doctor telling us we had lost. Since the blood condition causes clotting, I have always had to have the Rhesus factor needle (given to mothers who have blood conditions or whose blood type might be incompatible with their baby's blood type) after birth as well, so after finding out about our loss, the worst thing was having to trot down to the maternity ward at the hospital to have the needle. Cruel. I cried my eyes out that day, and have many times since.

The loss never leaves you. I wanted to remember our little one in some way that meant he was with us always. I had the photo that the ultrasound gave us and the pregnancy test indicator sewn into the belly of a teddy bear. That teddy sits in our room, up high. We have family stickers on our car – one sticker to represent every family member – and I got one for Oliver. It sits above the rest of us, and has a halo, to signify a lost baby. I don't care what people think, he was with us and he deserves to be thought of and seen.

Loss comes in so many ways, and grief takes us in so many ways. While writing this I have lost my mum, and have since found out after her passing that she gave birth to two sons that I had no idea about. She died at age 87, and I am heartbroken that she could never talk of them with me. Which makes it even more important that we celebrate their lives, even though they were so short. Babies are born with love and always will be.

        Maree - Brisbane Queensland

*"Our lives will be perfect when you're pregnant.
You'll never be able to leave me"*

When a Pregnancy is Unwanted

He was charming, funny, good-looking, attentive, and he swept me off my feet. If it was not love at first sight, it was close to it – and the feeling seemed to be mutual.

The first night we spent together he murmured as I drifted towards sleep, "I hope you're pregnant." I jerked awake. I didn't know what to say – as much as I liked this man, it was far too soon to be talking about children! I squeezed his hand under the blankets and went back to sleep.

Within three months I had moved in with him. He told me he couldn't stand to be without me at night, which I thought was sweet. He brought up the pregnancy issue again: "I'd really like you to get pregnant. At least then I'd know you wouldn't leave me."

"Don't be ridiculous," I said. "Why would I leave you?"

Some time after I'd moved in with him, I couldn't find my contraceptive pills. I turned the house upside down but they were nowhere to be found. He told me not to worry. I'd be able to get some more in a couple of days, right?

Later that month I began to feel sick in the mornings. I was tired all the time and my breasts hurt. I took a pregnancy test, already knowing the answer. He had got his way. He was delighted and rang everyone to tell them the news. "Now everyone knows I'm a real man," he said, which I thought was about the most stupid thing I'd ever heard.

I should have been happy, but I wasn't. I hadn't had a choice in this pregnancy. I felt physically wretched, but he would not lift a finger to help me. I began to feel increasingly isolated. We lived in the country and the nearest city was nearly an hour away through a mountain pass that was often closed during winter. I could not often see my friends or my family, and when I did, he insisted on being with me.

About two weeks after we had discovered I was pregnant I had what seemed to be a very heavy, painful period. The doctor confirmed I had a miscarriage. I was relieved and he was philosophical. "We'll try again," he said. Not if I could help it.

Shortly after this my contraceptive pills – which I had begun to take again after my miscarriage – disappeared again. This time, I knew he was responsible. But I could not get to the doctor within a couple of days. He phoned my work to tell them I was sick, hid the car keys from me, and forced me to have sex with him numerous times.

"Our lives will be perfect when you're pregnant again," he said. "You'll never be able to leave me."

My friends and workmates knew there was something not right with my situation, but I was too ashamed to tell anyone. And when I again fell pregnant, I gave up any pretence of fighting. This man had control of my life and I could do nothing about it.

I hate to think what my life might have become if it hadn't been for my best friend, Paul. Paul and I had barely seen each other since this relationship began because my partner was so jealous of him. But one Saturday afternoon Paul sent me a text message.

"I'm worried about you. Are you okay?" his text read. I turned my phone to silent and casually walked to the bathroom so my partner would not be suspicious.

"Not really."

"Are you afraid of him?"

"Yes. I want to leave but can't."

He asked me if we would be home that evening and I said yes. I warned him not to come to the house.

But that night Paul did turn up at our house. He had four friends with him. While his mates did the heavy on my partner, Paul and I grabbed as much of my stuff as we could and we all left. I never saw my partner again.

I lived at Paul's house for nearly a year, frightened that my partner would find me again. I was always looking over my shoulder. But Paul and his mates kept a constant eye on me and eventually I began to relax. It was at Paul's house, just a couple of weeks after my escape, that I again miscarried. My last tie to my partner was gone.

Looking back over the space of more than a decade, I feel sad about those two unknown, innocent creatures. I call them creatures because they were never babies to me. They were problems that made an awful situation worse. But they were alive – for a while – and they carried my DNA. They were as close to being a mother as I'll ever get; I wish I had been able to feel joy in their existence.

After that I decided I didn't want children. I'm now lucky enough to be married to a wonderful man, and I have two lovely stepdaughters and two snuggly little dogs. My life is good, and I'm grateful for it.

Anonymous - New Zealand

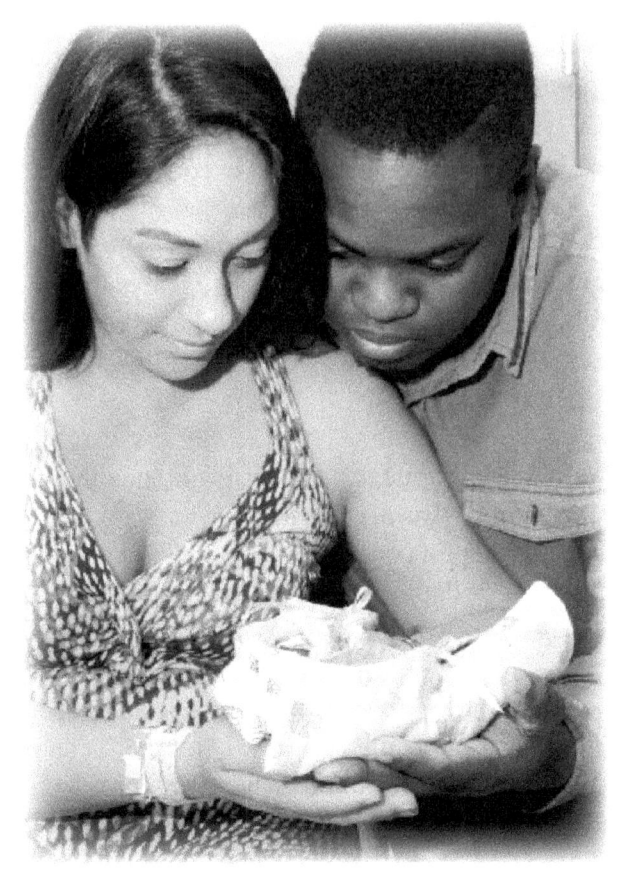

One Heart, Thrice Broken

It was one of the most beautiful images my husband and I have ever seen. I screamed "twins!!!" It was clear as day at my eight-week ultrasound appointment that there were two beautiful babies in my womb. After having an early miscarriage just six months prior we felt so blessed to be given not one, but two babies. Tears of happiness flowed as we stared in amazement at our two new blessings.

I was immediately sent to a maternal fetal medicine specialist (MFM) because of the type of twins my doctor presumed I was carrying. Which was confirmed when the doctor announced they were monochorionic diamniotic twins, identical twins sharing the same placenta and each baby was in its own amniotic sac. Both my OBGYN and MFM specialist would monitor me during my pregnancy.

Our families were overjoyed about the news of our twins. I beamed with pride, knowing I was carrying two precious little ones. A few weeks later we found out we were having boys. How amazing to add two more boys to our burgeoning all-male family. This would make baby boys three and four. My pregnancy was going absolutely wonderful. No morning sickness and very little fatigue. I was on cloud 9.

During a routine check-up with my doctor at 18 weeks, he noticed a very large discrepancy in the size of my twins, as well as an enlarged heart in one of the babies. We immediately scheduled an appointment with my MFM specialist to get specific details on the health of my boys.

After a very in-depth ultrasound, we were told that our boys had stage four twin-to-twin transfusion syndrome.
Twin-to-twin transfusion syndrome (TTTS) is when twins share unequal amounts of the placenta's blood supply because of abnormal blood vessel connections between the twins. The blood flow through these blood vessel connections become unbalanced, resulting in the two fetuses growing at different rates, in turn causing various medical conditions. One baby is called the "recipient" while the other baby is called the "donor". 70% of identical twins share a placenta, and 15-20% of these pregnancies are affected by TTTS. There are 5 stages of TTTS. Stage five is when one or both twins have passed.

Shock, anger, confusion, and sadness overtook me. How could this be? Why was this not caught sooner? My doctor went on to tell me there were only two options. First would be to do nothing at all and my twins would have a 100 percent mortality rate; or second would be to fly to Colorado and get an in-utero procedure done called fetoscopic laser ablation, to attempt to seal the abnormal blood vessels causing the TTTS. Of course the latter would be our only option; we would do anything to save our babies' lives! We chose to proceed with the fetoscopic laser ablation procedure, and had to move extremely quickly as the "recipient" baby had severe heart failure and could pass at any moment. Three hours later my husband and I were on a plane to Colorado.

We arrived in Colorado on a very frigid and sombre evening. Still in shock, we took what seemed to be a long and very quiet cab ride to the Children's Hospital of Colorado. I was immediately taken in for a series of tests to see just how extensive the TTTS was. My recipient baby, who was named Matias, had heart failure, hydrops, polyhydramnios and an 80 percent placental share. My donor baby, who was named Mael, was anemic, 30 percent smaller than his brother, had intrauterine growth restriction, oligohydramnios, and a mere 20 percent placental share. The following morning we were scheduled to complete the fetoscopic laser ablation procedure to save my babies.

Being wheeled into the operating room was like something out of a horror movie. The 20 staff members in their blue scrubs and masks surrounded me, classical music was playing throughout the operating room, while bright lights were shining in my face. I can remember the hum and beep of the multitude of medical equipment and machines that were hooked up to monitor me. I had never been so nervous, scared and fearful of what was to come. The medical staff had three lives in their hands and all we could do was pray for the best outcome.

The procedure was to only take an hour to complete, but ended up being a three-hour procedure. I was in and out of consciousness, and at one point towards the end of the procedure I woke up on the operating table. I vaguely remember hearing the doctors discussing my babies' heartbeats. The first thing I asked the anaesthesiologist who was sitting nearby was, are my babies OK? She told me my babies were both alive, but that the surgeon was unable to complete the procedure.

The doctors waited until I was completely awake to explain exactly what had happened. They told us that complications had arisen during the surgery. As soon as the doctors entered into my womb around my navel, I had myometrial bleeding at the entry site. They were not able to see the placenta clearly due to all of the bleeding.

They even tried to remove the foggy amniotic fluid by replacing it with clear fluid, but to no avail. Unfortunately, after several attempts, the doctors were unsuccessful in getting the amniotic fluid clear enough to proceed with the laser procedure.

Again, we had to quickly move forward and figure out our options. What was best for Matias and Mael? The doctors told us we had three options. The first was to do nothing and let nature take its course. My babies would soon pass away on their own. Second, would be selective reduction. We would have to sacrifice one of the twins to potentially save the other twin's life - they suggested we terminate our recipient baby, Matias. Lastly, we could try the laser ablation procedure one more time, the very next day. This option had far more potential complications since it had just been attempted, and the outcome was unsuccessful. However, the first and second options weren't even options for us. Who am I to decide whether to take the life of my own child? What kind of mother would I be if I didn't even attempt to try this procedure again? Without even needing time to think about our decision, I immediately told the doctors I wanted them to perform the procedure again.

Déjà vu? Groundhog Day, perhaps? There I was, the very next morning, being wheeled right back into that same cold, bright, blue scrub staff-filled, classical music-playing room. Again, what was supposed to take an hour, took three hours. Once the anaesthesia wore off, they told me that the second procedure was successful and that both babies were alive. They simply said that if anything bad were to happen to my twins, it would happen within the next 24 hours.

We were scheduled for an ultrasound the next morning. There was no doubt in my mind that everything was well and that Matias and Mael were thriving. The first baby the sonographer checked during the ultrasound was Matias, the recipient, and he had a strong and beautiful heartbeat. Within hours of the procedure Matias had already started to heal from his heart failure and hydrops. I immediately asked, "Is there a heartbeat on Mael?" The doctor paused for a moment and then began to explain the most horrific news an expectant mother and father could ever hear: "I'm sorry, but there is no heartbeat." I turned to look at my husband. All I can remember is shaking my head "no" vigorously with my legs flailing under the sheets. My husband kept saying, "No, I won't believe that." Eventually the staff exited the room, most likely deciding it would be best to leave and give us time alone.

During our alone time, there were no words spoken, how could there be, we were petrified. There was nothing to say at a moment such as this. Internally, I knew I had to continue to fight for the "survivor", Matias. I would still have to be strong and carry both babies until Matias was born.

We stayed in Colorado for six more days. After several echocardiograms, ultrasounds and MRI's, the doctors cleared me to fly back home. Matias continued to heal and became healthier every day. I was put on bed rest with only bathroom privileges until I gave birth. They feared that I would have preterm premature rupture of membranes(PPROM), because of the 6 incisions I had received during the two laser procedures. I often thought of the bittersweet day that I would give birth to my boys, knowing that only one had survived and the other would be born sleeping.

After two weeks of being on my strict bed rest I noticed a decrease in fetal movement with Matias. My husband and I immediately went to the hospital. They monitored his heart and we were cleared to go back home, as all seemed well. Two days passed, and as I was getting my oldest son ready for school, again, I felt no movement. Although I had a doctor's appointment that afternoon with my MFM specialist, they told me to come in immediately. As I was getting the ultrasound done, I asked the sonographer if she could see the baby's heartbeat. She said, "I'm having trouble finding it." She then left the room to find the doctor. As I waited for the doctor, tears immediately began to stream from my eyes. Moments later the doctor walked in and told us that Matias had passed away that night, as I was sleeping. I can't quite put my feelings into words. They were simply indescribable, the pain was unbearable.

The next morning I was scheduled to be induced and give birth to my twins. After a tearful, prayerful, and sleepless night we headed to the hospital. We had yet to tell our older sons what was happening. We told them while at the hospital, right before I was to be induced. My oldest was heartbroken, which ripped me to pieces even more.

On the 29th of October, 2014, after 13 long hours of labour, I gave birth to two beautifully perfect boys. Matias Yanai and Mael Nasir Johnson. They resembled their older brothers so much. They had perfect feet, the cutest hands and adorable button noses. Matias was big enough to cradle Mael in his arms. We spent one and a half days with our handsome boys, we bathed and put lotion on them, we held and loved on them. I even sang to them. My husband and I had portraits taken of the four of us. My pastor came and blessed them too. I didn't want our time together to end. I could have held them forever.

Planning and arranging for their cremation was just as difficult and painful. Instead of choosing what cute matching outfits to bring them home in, we had to quickly choose a funeral home that would be fulfilling the services we needed for our boys. We watched as the funeral home drove off and left with Matias and Mael, from the hospital. I had just given birth to two beautiful boys, yet I left with empty arms.

Matias and Mael opened the eyes of my heart. They allowed me to see the beauty in things I never knew were there. I will be forever changed. Missing them never ends, my love for them is everlasting. It will never grow old or ever fade away. They will always carry a piece of my heart with them in heaven.

As a mother of angel babies, one of my biggest fears is that our babies will be forgotten. I try my hardest to do things to honour Matias, Mael, and our early loss baby, whom we named Angel. My breast milk came in three days after having my twins. After giving it great thought, instead of stopping my milk I decided to pump and donate it. I found a local group that connects you with mothers who are in need of milk. I pumped religiously every three to four hours for three months. I donated my milk to a 10-month-old baby girl named Holly. Yes, at times I broke down, thinking to myself, This milk should be for my boys, but I'm using it for a baby that isn't even mine. In retrospect, I believe it was the best decision for me. It helped my healing process and most importantly, honoured my boys.

I am currently in the process of learning how to sew. All of the clothing that my boys have ever worn in and while leaving the hospital were either sewn or knitted and donated by either churches, individuals, or foundations. My plan is to make clothing for smaller babies, such as mine, and donate the clothing to the hospital where my babies were born.

For their first heavenly birthdays, we donated memory boxes to the hospital where my twins were born. We received the same memory boxes to take home when I gave birth to Matias and Mael. We tailored our boxes with items we find enjoyable: a journal, candles, candy, chapstick, keepsakes, a framed poem, a book, socks, a stuffed animal, and special toiletries for the new mother. We attached a small note saying they were donated in memory of our children.

I currently sit in the NICU with my 5-day-old rainbow baby, Silas. I am overcome with joy. He has already brought light and healing to our family. I want to tell all the mothers to be, mothers to come, and mothers whose children left this world way too soon, to never lose hope. Do not let fear steal your joy for the future. May God bless you on your journey and give you strength, comfort, peace and hope.

Shalina J - Phoenix, AZ USA

Nay-Nay, Our Early Arriver

I have a wonderful husband, who I've been with since we were 16 and two beautiful children. We have a son Bayley, who is eight years old and a daughter who is now six years old (going on 25!).

Our son was born on the 2nd of September 2007. I had a normal 38-week pregnancy, despite bad heartburn, horrible morning sickness and terribly, agonizing pelvic pain. Oh and that my labour was 22 hours long - on Fathers' Day! But I can't complain, as all went well.

I became pregnant with our daughter a year and a half later. My pregnancy was going great. I had my gynecologist appointment on the 28th of August 2009 and everything was perfect. I was told I could deliver the baby in about five week's time from that appointment. We were pretty excited.

We had a friend's birthday party on the 31st of August 2009. There was a jumping castle - of course my son was one of the first on it. He loves them! Lunch was ready to be served, and I went to get my son off the jumping castle, but being a kid he jumped off the jumping castle and into my arms. I thought nothing of it, as he always did that. I felt a slight pull in my lower abdomen, not painful at all. I forgot about it, as it didn't give me any trouble afterwards.

A few days later, on the 1st of September 2009, when I was 31.5 weeks pregnant, I was casually reading our soon-to-be two–year-old son a book. I felt a dull, heavy period-like ache in my lower abdomen and lower back. It took me by surprise, as I hadn't felt this ache much during this pregnancy. I got up quite quickly and as soon as I did, I felt a huge watery gush appear from me. I was wearing black pants, so I assumed my waters broke.

Standing in the hallway, I rang hubby straight away to come home. He was working about 40 minutes away from home. Had it been the day before he would have been only five minutes away – isn't that always the way?!

As soon as I went to the bathroom, I noticed it wasn't my waters. It was blood! So much of it, it looked pretty scary! Meanwhile, my son was in his room still looking at the book I had been reading him.

I stayed very calm, as I remembered if mum stays calm, so does baby. I rang emergency immediately. The emergency call operator was so lovely and kept me calm throughout the whole ordeal. Funny enough, I was in absolutely no pain what so ever.

She asked me where I was. I replied by saying I was sitting on the toilet as blood was gushing out like a tap. I didn't want to freak my son out if he saw what was happening! She told me that I have to get off the toilet as baby could be born any minute. At that point I kind of started to panic...but still kept myself quite calm for my son's and my unborn baby's sakes.

The operator asked me to get some towels; but I had no towels in the bathroom at that moment. I was running through the house, pouring blood (sorry for the graphic detail!). There were pools of blood throughout my house. It looked terrifying!

After what seemed like a long time but was actually about seven minutes, I heard the ambulance sirens. Thank goodness, thank goodness, I kept saying to myself. But of course the front door was locked. So holding the bloodied towel below , and hopping over to the front door as quickly as I could, I unlocked it to find two male ambulance guys standing there. I had no time to be embarrassed, I was just so grateful they were there to help my baby and me!

The ambulance of course caused a stir on my quiet street. One of my beautiful neighbour's came over to look after my son while I was rushed to the hospital, and then called my mother to stay with our son, which I am very grateful for. My neighbour also cleaned up after me, which she didn't have to do at all. I am forever grateful for all who helped me that day.

As the ambulance officers were putting me on the stretcher, I was asked which hospital I preferred, Blacktown or Mt Druitt. I had a bad experience with Blacktown years before, so I was very hesitant to go there. They persuaded me to go to Blacktown, as I was going to have this baby in 10 minutes!

As soon as I was lying in the back of the ambulance, I started getting contractions, and pretty strong ones too. This baby of ours was obviously ready to make her entrance. On my way to the hospital, while being checked over by the lovely ambulance officers, all I could think was, Please let my baby be healthy.

When I arrived at the hospital I was rushed in to have an emergency caesarean. My hubby was nowhere in sight although – unknown to me - he was rushing to get to us like a crazy man.

Some of the staff did not seem very friendly. My nail polish had to be removed for the emergency caesarian, and I made a small joke to the nurse removing it: "Oh, you get the fun job." She rolled her eyes and totally ignored me. I said out loud, "Geez, anyone would think that you're the one on the surgery table!" Maybe it wasn't the time or place to joke around, but that's just how I am. I was desperate to see my husband, but he arrived 10 minutes after I was taken into theatre.

I was devastated that my husband missed the birth of our baby. I was given a full anesthetic, so I couldn't say how long I was out for or even who performed the surgery. When I finally awoke, I had no idea if my baby was OK or not. They had put me in a room with no windows or anything and the lights were very dimmed. I called for a nurse to take me to see my baby. I know how busy nurses are, so I completely understand why they didn't rush to me. But for me, this was a huge deal! I desperately wanted to meet my baby and just know that she was ok.

Finally after 15-20 minutes, a nurse came in and abruptly responded, "What do you want?" I couldn't believe how rude they were to me after the ordeal I had just gone through. Meanwhile, as I was waiting for someone to take me to see my daughter, I heard the staff laughing and joking around right outside my door. It was unbelievable.

At this stage, the doctor came in and told me that I had placenta abruption. I had read so much about placenta abruption, but I never thought it would happen to me! The doctor said to me that it usually only happens to people who are heavy smokers, drug users and alcoholics! I don't ever touch any of those things, so they can throw that theory out the window.

The nurse finally took me to see our daughter. The first person I saw was my amazing husband. I just cried when I saw him. He had actually met our daughter before I did. We went in together for me to meet our beautiful baby girl for the first time. After seeing my little princess covered in tubes and wires, lying there helpless in the humidity crib, we just didn't know what to expect.

Being wheeled in, pale and weak as I was, I met our beautiful daughter. I fell in love the moment I saw her. We named her Shonaya. Despite all the tubes and wires attached to her, she was perfect. She did need a little help with breathing, so she needed the CPAP. Shonaya weighed 1.7kgs. She was so tiny. But overall she was a good weight to be at eight weeks' premature, which was in her favour. And boy, she had a set of lungs on her!
We weren't allowed to hold our precious baby as yet. So we did miss out on a lot of things, such as photos of her birth, being able to hear her cry for the first time, giving her, her first sip of breast milk and even just holding her. But she was in great care.

So just after five minutes of meeting Shonaya, of course there was always one nurse who had to be quite blunt. While the nurse was leaning on the humidity crib where my daughter lay, she gazed at me and said very abruptly, "Now you know she could possibly die, don't you?" I looked at her and didn't know what to say, my eyes filled with tears. I was gobsmacked! I think we all knew that it was a possibility, but all I kept thinking was positive vibes. I didn't want a person like that around my baby!

A head nurse approached me and asked what happened as another nurse overheard the conversation. I told her what was said. I clearly stated that I believe people with attitudes like that should not be in positions of caring for other people who are unwell or who have been through traumatic situations.

I know nurse's jobs are huge and have a great deal of significance in our communities. I have so much respect for doctors and nurses, but only the ones who have compassion, sympathy and thoughtfulness towards their patients. It's called humanity. Unfortunately, many people lack of.

I'm not sure what happened after that, as all I was concerned about was our daughter. I was taken back to the dimmed room, which made me feel uneasy. A nurse came in and without giving me any local anesthetic, pulled out my catheter out there and then. I was in so much pain that I grabbed her hand and said some unsavoury words. Not meaning to be rude to the nurse, but the pain I was in was worse than natural labour!

Most of it is a blur after that traumatic ordeal. The next thing I remember is being taken to RPA hospital by ambulance to spend the next two weeks with our baby girl. My husband said that they were going to send us to Melbourne if they couldn't find us a bed in Sydney. Thankfully they did!

Once we arrived at RPA, I wasn't feeling my usual self. I was quite depressed and missing my husband and our son so much. Being alone in a place where you know no-one can be pretty daunting. I had to share a room where the lady didn't speak a word of English, so it made it so hard to make a friend while there.

I clearly remember the lady I was sharing a room with had brought in her other children who were sick with the flu into my room also. So that made me quite nervous, as I was frightened Shonaya would become unwell.

I was sad all the time. I just didn't want to be there. But I was so grateful for all the nurses and doctors who were looking after our baby girl. I just wanted to be home with my new baby, son and husband.

One of the counsellors came to speak to me. She allowed me go home on the weekends. This was such a huge relief for me, but I was constantly crying because I just felt so down and hated leaving my baby there without me.

After two weeks I started feeling better, although I was still in pain from the C-section.
We were then transferred to Norwest private hospital in Bella Vista, our daughter's home for another two weeks. With help from my husband, mother and mother-in-law driving me back and forth for feeding times, I was in much better spirits and Shonaya was doing so well.

Every day our daughter was improving and getting bigger and stronger. It was such a great feeling! After two weeks, Shonaya was able to come home, even though she was still so small at just 36 weeks' gestation. I was quite strict about having any visitors at this point, as I was afraid of Shonaya becoming unwell. We were just over the moon that after all our little family went through; we came out stronger in the end, especially our little Shonaya.

Shonaya is now seven years old and full of laughs, attitude and lots of energy! The way it should be.

I know so many mothers and fathers don't have the same outcome that we did. So I would like to send all my love, strength, positive energy and support to all who are going through such hard times and heartache with pregnancy/birth related issues. I wish each and every person reading this the very best outcome in becoming parents. Never give up.

        Martina Vassallo - Sydney Australia

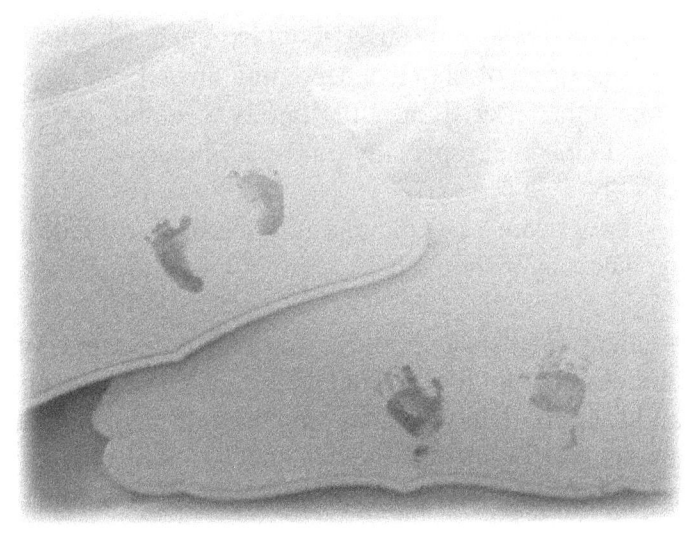

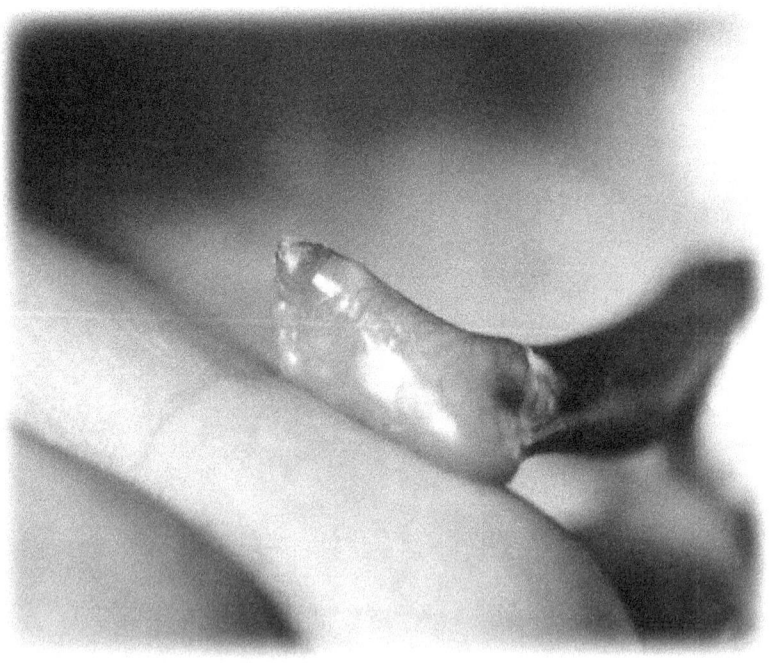

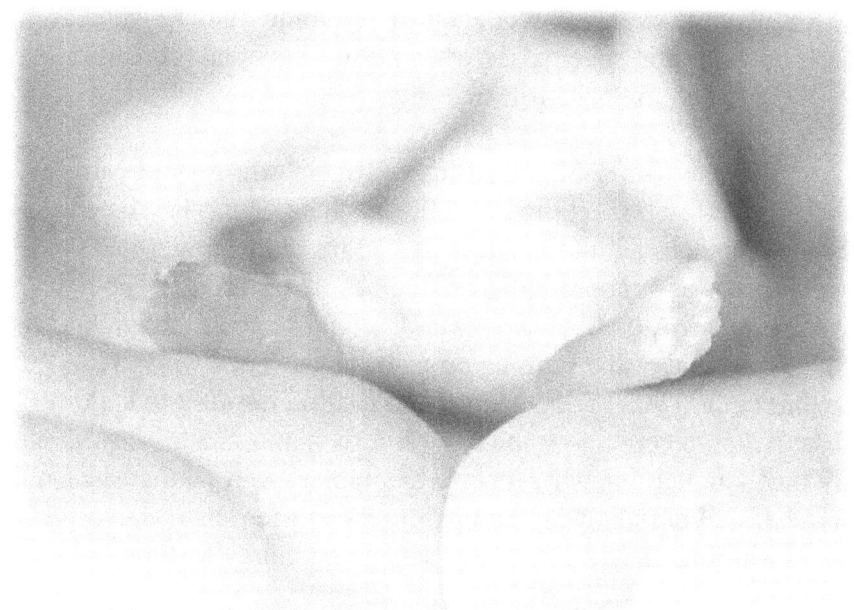

Ava Grace-Birth Story

The staff assigned for Ava's birth are some of the most compassionate people I have ever met.

They pass the tissues as I cry hysterically about how unfair this all is. They listen as I let out a gut-wrenching roar from deep within about not even eating a piece of deli meat or seafood this pregnancy. They hold my hand and agree with me that this is the worst situation you can be in. They run and grab me vomit bags time and time again and agree that it shouldn't have been that I have also had to go through hyperemesis gravidarum for the entire pregnancy, yet don't get to hold a warm, wriggling baby in the end. They hold my hand as they give me needles and other medications to help with the relentless nausea, which is a combination of extreme fear, panic, sadness, shock, morning sickness and morphine.

They bring my husband meals, which he cannot eat, but we are grateful for the gesture. They tell me I can do this, that I am strong, that I will get to meet my daughter soon. They say her name, her beautiful name over and over again. They come running when I push my button in sheer panic when my waters break, screaming for them to call my obstetrician.

They calm me with soothing words and again affirm that I can do this, that I will meet my precious daughter soon. They listen through my sobs about the plans we had for our daughter and our family that was supposed to have five people in it soon.. They check me calmly as I begin to enter the final stage of labour, knowing that the end of the birthing process is near. They whisper to my husband to quickly go and tell the staff on the desk to call my obstetrician to come now, the baby's birth is imminent! They hold my tiny daughter for what feels like hours in a way so that she isn't born before I am ready and not before the obstetrician arrives. As we are waiting, they describe my daughter's dainty features.

The obstetrician arrives. He is the same one who delivered my son and older daughter over the past few years; in my eyes he is the best obstetrician in the world. Calmly he delivers my third child. Her birth is silent. The room is silent. There are no tears. There are no cheers. The obstetrician describes in detail what she looks like, asking gently if we want to see her. My husband and I look at each other with a glance, both knowing the answer in that second. Yes please, we want to see her, we want to hold her and never let her go. We want to cuddle her, and love on her and kiss her. I am handed her, all 15.5cm and 105 grams, to hold after a 2.5-hour labour.

I'm exhausted, emotionally and physically, but I'm smiling, I'm actually grinning ear to ear, just as if I'd given birth to a full term, healthy baby. I am in such awe about what a perfectly formed little girl we have created. I am so happy to meet her and hold her.

At the same moment that my heart is being shattered into a million pieces, my heart is also full. My husband reaches out to touch her. I see the deep pain but also so much love for our third child. The midwife and obstetrician have tears in their eyes and comment how beautiful she is. She really is beautiful.

Ava died because of fatal birth defects. We have heard the term 'incompatible with life' said many times before and after her birth, but those words (which I hate) don't take away anything from her beauty. They don't take away from the fact that she always had a place in our family. That she was supposed to be born.

How amazing, that at 15.3 weeks gestation she has 10 tiny fingers and toes. She has her sister's chin, she has her daddy's toes, she has her brother's fingers, and she has my knees. Her knuckles are all there and her fingernails are formed. Two tiny ears, two tiny eyes and a perfect little mouth. Just a tiny baby. Our baby.
AVA GRACE JOHNSON. Monday 16th March 2015.
Born still, but still born.

Psalm 139:13-16 (NIV)
For you created my inmost being; you knit me together in my mothers womb. I praise you because I am fearfully and wonderfully made; your works are wonderful, I know that full well. My frame was not hidden from you when I was made in the secret place, when I was woven together in the depths of the earth. Your eyes saw my unformed body; all the days ordained for me were written in your book before one of them came to be.

Erin and Mathew Johnson – Western Sydney, Australia
babyjcystichygroma.blogspot.com.au

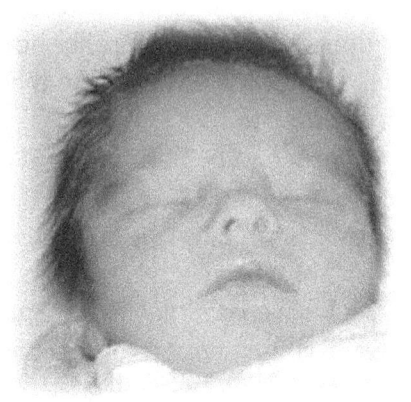

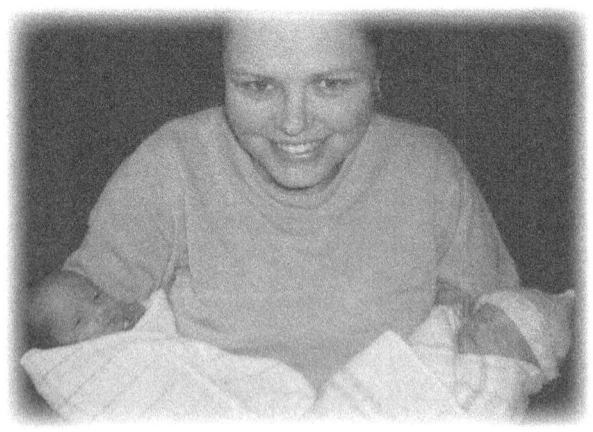

Our Precious Twins Complete our Family

It was our son James' first birthday. We had decided that once he turned one that we would try for baby number two, as we wanted a fairly close age gap. It had taken us about six months to fall pregnant with James.

It had been a normal pregnancy besides the horrendous morning sickness that stayed with me for the whole pregnancy. James was born via spontaneous labour at 35 weeks. I was still working as a teacher at the time, and had another two weeks of work before my maternity leave started. He was born, after a 14-hour labour and a vacuum extraction, weighing a healthy 2780g. James spent five days in the SCN (Special Care Nursery) and was initially being tube fed. On the fourth day he learned to suck feed and was able to come home.

Months went by and there was no positive pregnancy test. I saw my doctor who referred me to an obstetrician. I was diagnosed with PCOS after having some tests and the doctor said that we are most likely to need some help to fall pregnant. We decided to give it a few more months and did everything possible to help our chances. We changed our diet drastically and ate a very healthy balanced diet, including fish and nuts. We exercised daily and both lost over 20kg of weight. We took vitamin supplements and followed every old wives' tale, took on every bit of advice; but still no luck. The doctor prescribed me metformin and clomid to ensure I ovulated every month, as the blood tests had shown that wasn't always the case. I continued taking them for four months, with no success. I then tried acupuncture for fertility, which was successful in making me ovulate, but not fall pregnant.

After 18 months we were referred to the Sydney IVF clinic. We were hesitant to go, but we would have done anything to get a brother or sister for James. We went along to the appointment worried and nervous. The obstetrician referred us to "the best IVF doctor" as he said, and even though he was an hour away from us, we were willing to try. After doing some tests and an ultrasound of both me and my husband, we were told that it was highly unlikely that we would be able to conceive naturally. He gave us only a 2 per cent chance.

We left the appointment disheartened but determined to keep trying. As 2 per cent was better than 0 per cent we decided we would continue trying for another six months on our own, before beginning the IVF process.

This was a bit of a relief for us. We relaxed a bit. We knew that if in six months I was not pregnant, we would go back to the IVF clinic and begin the process. I think your emotional state plays a big part in the conception process. Because three months later, a home pregnancy test confirmed I was pregnant. All on our own! No help needed.

I went to my GP, who did a blood test to confirm the pregnancy.

When the results were back, she said to me, "You are either a lot further along than four weeks or you are having twins. Your HCG levels are quite high." I jokingly laughed and told her that I was sure of my dates, but there couldn't possibly be more than one baby.

From four weeks onwards, I was constantly nauseous and sick. I was vomiting up to 10 times a day and couldn't even keep down water. I ended up going to the emergency department at the hospital twice because I was so dehydrated. Each time, they admitted me and put me on a drip of fluids and Maxolon, rehydrated me and then sent me home. I had to come back daily after being sent home for a few hours a day on a drip.

I had an appointment with my obstetrician when I was seven weeks pregnant. He was happy for us, as we hadn't needed to take the IVF route. He had an ultrasound machine in his room, and did an ultrasound, hoping to see a sac and a heartbeat. Before the ultrasound he said to us, "The last two patients of mine today have found out that they are having twins. I wonder if you will be the third?" We laughed and said "Yeah yeah, as if that would happen to us!" Once the ultrasound started I immediately saw two distinct sacs on the screen. He shook my husband's hand and said, "Congratulations, you are having twins." We were in disbelief. How could this be? We could only laugh and tell him there must be a problem with his machine. But it was true, we were having twins! All on our own!

The pregnancy was a difficult one. I was diagnosed with hyperemesis gravidarum, as my morning sickness was so severe. I had to take eight weeks' sick leave from work as there was no way I could teach a class without running out multiple times a day to vomit. I was also diagnosed with gestational diabetes and had to be monitored through the high risk clinic at the hospital because of a multiple birth, previous premature birth and diabetes.

The ultrasound confirmed we were having Dichorionic/Diamniotic (di/di) twins. Di/di twins are the most common type of twins and the lowest risk. Di/di twins can be identical if the egg split very early, but fraternal twins are always di/di. Our twins were fraternal di/di twins; each twin had their own placenta and their own amniotic sac. Di/di twin pregnancies have increased risks over single pregnancies, but this is the best case scenario in twin world. The biggest worry was going into preterm labour and making sure both babies were growing adequately.

My aim was always to get to 34 weeks, so I could deliver at my local hospital and so my babies would have the best chance of survival. At 32 weeks six days I went into labour. I was having contractions and I was 2cm dilated. I went to the hospital, which confirmed that I was in labour. But they told me I could not have the babies there, as there were too many premature babies to be cared for. They told me that they would ring around to find the closest hospital that has available beds. A short while later they said that they had two beds in Canberra. I asked them to keep trying, as I wanted to stay in Sydney if possible. They came back to me and said they had one NICU bed in Liverpool and one in Royal North Shore, so I could deliver at Liverpool, but one baby would be sent to the other hospital. That wasn't good enough, and after persisting with them, they got two NICU beds in Liverpool. They put me in an ambulance and transferred me to Liverpool, and gave me tocolytic drugs to stop the labour. The drugs worked. Labour stopped and everything seemed good.

They kept me in hospital for 24 hours and then sent me home. We thought we had escaped a premature birth. WRONG! A few hours after getting home, my waters broke in bed. They were on their way. This time I went straight to Liverpool. They gave me a shot of steroids and an anti D injection for my negative rhesus blood type.

I laboured for 12 hours and then was so exhausted that I could not go on. I decided to have an epidural and it was heaven. I finally felt like I was in control and knew what was going on. At 4:45pm, the first twin, Harrison, was born. By this stage I had an audience of 11 people in the room! An obstetrician, two midwives, two pediatricians, two pediatric nurses and four students, plus us! Harrison was born and needed to be rubbed up before he cried. He was shown to me and then taken away to the neonatal intensive care nursery. I was told he was fine and weighed 2040g.

The second twin, Emily, was in no hurry to come at all. She was high up under my ribs and her water had not broken. The midwife broke her waters, and then tried to physically push her down into the birth canal. After 38 minutes of contractions and pushing, Emily was finally born at 5:23pm. She was wrapped up and taken away to NICU as well. She weighed a tiny 1890g.

Harrison and Emily both spent 24 hours on CPAP (Continuous positive airway pressure) to help with breathing, then three days in a humid crib. They were tube fed and had some trouble regulating their body temperature. After four days, they were transferred via ambulance from the NICU at Liverpool to the SCN at Campbelltown Hospital. They spent three weeks here, growing and learning to suck feed. It was a difficult time, having three-year-old James to look after, as well as spending days and nights at the hospital.

After three weeks, the twins were finally home. Our family was complete, and the fun was just starting! The first 12 months were difficult. They both had reflux, screamed lots and didn't sleep much. Emily was diagnosed with renal kidney reflux so had a few hospital stays and medical appointments that kept us busy.

But we are a family, and we are over the moon with happiness!

Alicia Sinfield - South-West Sydney, Australia

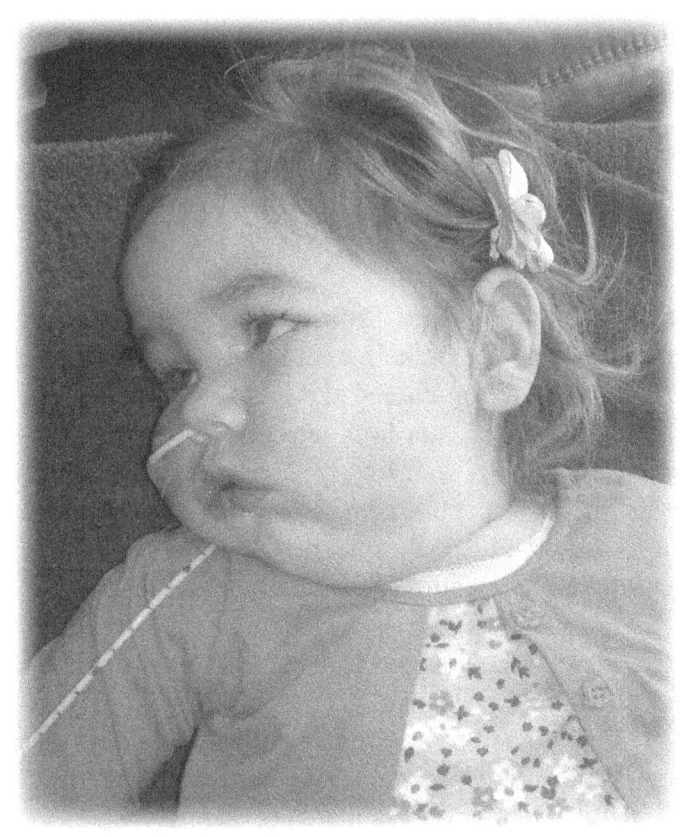

The Storm after the Rainbow

When I was 19 years old I was diagnosed with polycystic ovary syndrome (PCOS). The biggest thing to come out of that for me was that I would likely need medical assistance to get pregnant. Fifteen years later I got married. My husband and I had been together for six years by then but we didn't want to think about babies until we got married. So within months of our wedding I had an appointment with a fertility specialist. She was great and got us started straight away, using ovulation induction. It took probably six months but finally I was pregnant with my precious baby. I decided to wait until after the 12 week mark to tell my family, which coincided with a reunion of sorts as we were spread all over the country.

The day of our 12-week scan arrived and I was so excited to see my baby again (I'd seen him as a blob at seven weeks). Our excitement turned to fear when we were told that there was a mass in his abdomen. We were referred to the foetal medicine unit (FMU) at the hospital. They did more scans and told us the mass was a cyst but there was a good chance it would go away on its own. When we told our family there was excitement because we were having a baby, but also trepidation, as it wasn't going to plan. At 15 weeks I had what was supposed to be an amniocentesis but became a CVS (a similar test to an amniocentesis but a sample of the placenta is taken for testing, rather than a sample of amniotic fluid). I'll be honest and admit that it hurt. But it was all going to be worth it to find out what was going on with my baby.

After a long wait, we were given the news that the cyst had grown, and we were given the choice to terminate. I felt like I was giving up on the baby so we kept going with the pregnancy, with weekly scans. At least if I made it to 20 weeks he would be considered a legal person and would get a birth certificate.

Every week we had a scan and every week the cyst grew. My levels of amniotic fluid started to decline. I begged them to just inject me with more fluids. I drank more water in the hopes that would make a difference. But the fluid levels just kept dropping. Finally at 23 weeks, when there was barely any amniotic fluid left, we made the decision that no parent wants to make. Every week I had secretly hoped that he would have passed away so I wouldn't be the one to make the decision to terminate. I gave my work one day's notice that I was leaving for my maternity leave. I wouldn't be back for four months. There were no happy farewells and messages of luck. There were sad faces and hushed tones.

The next day we arrived at the hospital, which was blessedly quiet. We were put in the room designated for cases like ours, which had a double bed. It was the furthest away from all the other delivery rooms. I think this was the only time my husband openly cried for our baby. I was given the drugs for the induction and then we waited for our baby.

At 3.45am on 14 December, 2009 Charlie was born. There was no sign of life. I'm sure I felt him kick the night before so I don't know when he passed away. I can only hope that he was at peace.

It's only after two other pregnancies that I was able to recognise what I had felt as Charlie's kicking. Sometimes this gives me comfort and other times I question whether I made the right decision.

Charlie was quickly taken away so when I next saw him he was dressed in a little gown. He had black hands and feet from having his hand and footprints taken for us. We spent as much time with him as we could, and then when I left the hospital without him I wanted to scream at them to bring him back because I had changed my mind.

A post mortem revealed that there was so much that had gone wrong with Charlie's development. But we were told it was "just one of those things" and was unlikely to re-occur.

Because it was almost Christmas and so many of our family lived interstate, we decided to have a funeral with just the two of us. This was my first mistake as nobody else got the chance to say goodbye and we didn't get the support we needed from those close to us. In a way that likely made him less 'real'. My second mistake was continuing on with our plan of spending Christmas with family, the same family who didn't get to meet Charlie or say goodbye. I felt isolated and let down as those around me didn't talk about it because they didn't want to upset me. In hindsight, my husband and I should have taken the opportunity to check out of the world for a week or so to grieve properly.

As soon as the Christmas break was over I made another appointment with the fertility specialist. I was desperate to get pregnant again. This time it only took a couple of months before we found out I was pregnant. My rainbow baby would be due within days of Charlie's birthday!

At six weeks, after one of my regular blood tests, the doctor's receptionist commented that my HCG levels were high and maybe it was twins. This should have freaked me out but for some reason I had a feeling it was twins before she had said it. One week later a scan confirmed two little heartbeats. It almost felt like the scales were being balanced. We were already booked in to see an obstetrician who specialised in high-risk pregnancies, based on our experience with Charlie. So now we had two reasons to see her.

For the most part my pregnancy went without a hitch. I developed gestational diabetes but it was managed with diet initially, then with insulin. I had two placentas in there so the doctor wasn't surprised that insulin was needed. At the 20-week scan we found out we were having two girls. My husband later asked the OB to check again just in case. He grew up with only brothers so the idea of two girls terrified him!

At 30 weeks I was hospitalised with an extreme case of gastro, which was exacerbated by the diabetes. I was given steroid injections just in case the babies had to come out early.

Then at around 34 weeks I came down with some sort of mystery allergy. I was covered in hives and swelled up. I was again hospitalised so they could keep an eye on me. An ultrasound showed that one of the babies was starting to get distressed. At 3am I was told that the babies were coming out in the morning and I was given a tour of the Special Care Nursery (SCN) so I knew what to expect. I wasn't able to tell my husband until the morning and he almost didn't make it in time, as he didn't hear his phone at home!

At 10.07am Ruby was born weighing 2.1kg. At 10.08am Ashley was born weighing 2.5kg and needing a little bit of breathing assistance. Both were whisked away to the SCN before I could see them. Once I was back in my room I was told that Ruby would be brought in to visit. I was still numb from the epidural so was unable to go to the SCN myself. They brought her in all wrapped up in a blanket. I'd never even held a baby before so I was nervous to say the least. We didn't even unwrap her, as we weren't sure if we were allowed.

The next day I was able to go to the SCN and meet Ashley for the first time. The girls were in the nursery for three weeks before we were able to take them home. I was discharged after five days so leaving the hospital with empty arms again was emotional. There were many tears in the following days and weeks as I managed expressing breast milk with visiting the girls and trying to get breastfeeding established. I started to dread going in as we weren't having any luck and it was becoming distressing for all of us. When I confessed to one of the midwives how I felt she suggested trying a bottle. It was onwards and upwards from there and soon they were ready to come home.

In many ways my babies healed my heart but I have always tried my best to keep Charlie's memory alive, which can be hard when it feels like you're the only one who remembers. When the girls are older I will tell them all about their older brother.

When the twins were around 12 months old my husband suggested that I might have depression. I saw my GP and she prescribed anti-depressants and gave me a plan around counselling. I started seeing a counsellor and realised that I hadn't fully grieved for Charlie. My desire for a baby meant I hadn't allocated enough time to feel what I needed to feel.

Life with twins was very busy but when the dust finally started to settle we decided we wanted to add to our family. Off we went again to the fertility specialist. She kept a closer eye on things to make sure we didn't get twins again. It didn't take long before I was pregnant again. I returned to the same OB, even though this wasn't considered a high-risk pregnancy.

At 12 weeks the tests showed a high ratio for Down syndrome so at 15 weeks I underwent another amnio. This time it didn't hurt at all! The tests came back showing that everything was fine and we were having a little boy. We were so happy and I relinquished all of the girls' clothes that I had been saving.

The 20-week scan showed everything was developing normally. The doctor couldn't see the penis but wasn't concerned. He was just in a bad position. Every subsequent scan I asked again and he was always in a bad position. I expressed concern to my best friend and she bet me $1,000 that he would be born with a penis. Fast forward to 37 weeks and it seems I now had too much amniotic fluid. So it was decided to evict. At 3.18pm on 22 May my baby girl was born.

What? A girl? Everyone was surprised, including the OB. While I was still on the table from the caesarian section she showed me the report from the amnio, which said "XY chromosomes". I'm still waiting for my money from my friend's bet!

Once again my baby was taken away to the SCN before I could see her. This time though, my bed was taken into the nursery so I could see her. She couldn't be taken out of her crib as they were pumping in extra oxygen to help her breathing. It took us three days to decide on the name – Laura.

I was later told that Laura had a seizure when she was born and the doctors were concerned. An ultrasound was done on her brain and it showed some worrying signs of extra fluid in her brain. An MRI was done when she was just seven days old. She was a perfect patient and slept through the whole thing.

It was days later when we were given the news. Her brain hadn't developed properly and they weren't sure how she would be affected but it was unlikely she would walk. My OB came in and gave us her opinion. The worst-case scenario would be that Laura's condition was degenerative and we would lose her at a young age. So my baby was barely a week old and I found myself grieving for the life she wasn't going to get. Every time I looked at my beautiful baby I didn't feel joy, only sadness. It didn't seem fair that this was happening to our family, again. Hadn't we already had our share of heartache?

At four weeks of age Laura had her first hospital admission with bronchiolitis. It was the first of many and she became well known to the nurses in the paediatric ward.

At around nine months of age an EEG showed that Laura was having seizures, known as infantile spasms. She was immediately admitted to hospital and placed on steroids. Once they were under control she became a different baby. We went from having a baby who cried for hours every single night to a baby who didn't cry at all. My poor baby must have been in so much pain! I now had a very relaxed baby who only cried if something was really bothering her. Now when she cried we paid attention.

She spent her first birthday - and many other special events – in hospital. In the early months we also had appointments with endocrinologists, neurologists, hearing tests, eye tests and we began physiotherapy.

While Laura was in hospital for the seizures another MRI of her brain was performed. It showed our worst fears – Laura's brain was degenerating. It wasn't until Laura was over 12 months old that we were given a diagnosis – Pontocerebellar hypoplasia (PCH) type 7. PCH is a group of related conditions that affect the development of the brain, mainly the cerebellum. The 'type 7' indicates the condition also affected the sexual development of the child. It's likely that Laura was the only one in the country with PCH type 7. Now that I had a name I was able to find an online support group and I finally felt some hope – not that Laura would get better, but that at least we were no longer alone.

It seems Laura's case was mild with regards to seizures as we were able to control them. But with regards to her lack of development it was severe. She didn't advance developmentally beyond being a newborn, although she grew tall (and heavy). She wasn't even able to hold up her own head.

We were then set up under the care of a palliative care unit, who gave Laura regular checks at home. We continued her physiotherapy and organised mobility equipment as the need arose.

When Laura was around 18 months old she was again admitted to hospital with pneumonia. She got steadily worse and the treatment was not bringing any improvement. The doctor advised us that it was time to consider letting her go. All of our family arrived to say their goodbyes. We had no idea how to explain this to our girls, who weren't yet four years old.

Laura's room was rearranged to allow both my husband and I to stay with her. Her oxygen was removed and we waited for our baby girl to deteriorate. Only she didn't. Two days later we decided to take her home. A week later we had a visit from the doctor in the palliative care team and discovered her chest was clearer. She had improved! We met with the doctors and social workers and formed a plan for future treatment. One of the hardest decisions we made was to sign a Do Not Resuscitate order. We made the most of Laura's time with us, while trying to manage life with the twins and their new preschool routine. We were lucky enough that we were able to have a big birthday party for her second birthday, to make up for missing out on celebrating her first birthday.

Laura did not communicate, other than crying. She rarely made eye contact. In fact we weren't even sure how well she could see. But somehow I knew that she knew me and that she loved me. I never went back to work after Laura was born as I didn't want to spend any more of her short life away from her than was necessary. But in some ways I was delusional as there is always regret and "if only". If only I had sung to her more. If only we had taken her out and about more and given her experiences. If only I had taken more photos. This is my biggest regret. At the time there wasn't much on a day-to-day basis that seemed worthy of photos but now that she is gone I wish I had taken a photo every single day.

We were given a bonus 11 months with Laura before she caught yet another cold, which inevitably developed into pneumonia. Her lungs had never fully recovered from the bout that nearly killed her. We had previously decided that we weren't going to have hospital intervention when she got sick. That doesn't mean we denied her care. We put her on antibiotics and organised to have oxygen for her at home. I didn't think the oxygen would be enough to save her this time but she had surprised us so many times before that I needed to give her a chance. She did improve when we started the oxygen and even seemed well enough for my husband to go interstate to go to a concert he had bought tickets for six months earlier.

How wrong we were. She went downhill so quickly and now I was on my own and scared. I rang the palliative care team for advice but they didn't answer. I had another number to call if it was an emergency but it still didn't feel like one. I called a friend who had been Laura's respite nurse. I was unsure about giving her too much morphine as I knew while it would ease her distress it could also hamper her respiration. Her comfort was of most importance so I gave her morphine as she needed. But did I give her too much? I'll never know. As it got late I took her to bed with me. I was so tired and wanted her to sleep too. I sang to her all the songs she knew.

Her last moments were the most precious, as I held her in my arms and told her I loved her. I listened as the time between breaths increased until there were no more. I was all alone and my husband was on his way back from his concert, unaware of what was going on. I couldn't tell him while he was on the road. He arrived home 45 minutes after she left us. I'm sure she was tired from months of working so hard just to breathe, and I hope that she is now at peace.

Laura's funeral was everything it should have been. I tried to make up for not giving Charlie a proper send-off and I made sure to include everything in the ceremony that I wanted, regardless of what anyone else thought.

I even had my wedding dress made into a gown for Laura as another way to feel connected to her. She looked like an angel. It was a beautiful send-off and we had so much support from family and friends. Some friends I had never met before, as we had only known each other through online support groups. What a contrast this was to Charlie's farewell.

The twins coped remarkably well with Laura's passing. They saw Laura before the funeral home came and took her away and they helped cut some of Laura's hair as a keepsake and make handprints. I try my best to be honest with them about everything and we talk about Laura a lot. I bought a beautiful book about having a sister in heaven and it really resonates with them as the description of the funeral is almost exactly as we had for Laura.

Our first Christmas without Laura was difficult, especially as the girls requested to put Laura's Santa sack under the tree too. If it weren't for the twins and their excitement over Christmas I would have skipped it altogether. Not long after Christmas we received what I believe was a beautiful sign from Laura when a butterfly came by and sat on Ruby's head and then moved to Ashley's. Maybe it was merely coincidence, but it made us all feel like we had been visited by our beautiful girl and brought smiles to our faces.

Three months after Laura's passing we received news that the genetics team was able to identify the gene responsible for Laura's (and most likely Charlie's) condition. Now that they knew what it was we could test for it in future pregnancies. I knew my husband wanted another baby but I wasn't sure I could cope with another loss. But the more I thought about it and the more I saw babies in the street, I knew I wanted to try again.

Unfortunately my age was a significant hurdle and I felt that I did not have time to wait. Shouldn't I wait until I finish grieving for Laura? But that will take a lifetime. Nobody ever finishes grieving. They just learn to adapt to having a piece (or pieces) of their heart missing. I know this from my grief for Charlie. But Laura feels different. She was such an important part of our lives for the two years, two months and three and a half days she was with us. She isn't so easy to adapt to living without.

So I returned to the fertility specialist, who was quick to point out that, at 40 years old, I was less likely to have success. We decided that best plan for us was to conceive and then test the baby at 12 weeks. I almost needed to stay detached from the baby until we got past that test. Harden my heart to it so that if termination were necessary I wouldn't fall apart.

A few days before Christmas, after our first cycle, I felt triumphant as I got a positive pregnancy test. But the timing was awful as my specialist was closed for Christmas break. I went to a GP to get a blood test, as instructed. I couldn't see my regular GP as he had already gone on leave. The results came back positive, but the hormone levels were on the low side. Turns out, this GP was closed until January so in order to get a follow-up test done I had to go to yet another GP. I felt like a hypochondriac doing the rounds to get a diagnosis I wanted. I got the results from the second test and my hormone levels had risen but not as they should. The GP made no comment, even though the report showed the first week's results also. So then I could do nothing but wait.

New Year's Eve came and I broke down. 2015 had been the year where the worst thing that could happen to a person actually happened. But saying farewell to 2015 felt like I was casting my baby girl aside. Time was moving on without her. Plus I had to face the likely demise of this new pregnancy. Given what we had been through, I felt like I should have been bulletproof. Isn't that how karma works? Or am I being punished for trying to replace my baby girl? I know it's too soon but time is not on my side. Every day I ask for her forgiveness. But what I really need is to forgive myself and allow myself to continue living, for my sake and for my family's sake.

Crying on New Year's Eve almost cleansed me of any attachment to the pregnancy. I stopped worrying, as there was nothing I could do. My specialist finally returned and a new blood test showed my hormones had risen, but still not sufficiently. I knew it was over but she prescribed progesterone to try and give it a boost. I couldn't get out of my head though what all the experts say, that if it struggles then there is likely something wrong on a chromosome level. Given what I'd been through with Charlie and Laura I didn't want to fight for this one when my intuition told me that it wasn't right. So I felt relief when another blood test showed my hormones had started to decline and it was officially over. I wouldn't be put in a position of having to make another life or death decision for my child.

It's only been six months since we lost Laura so the grief is still quite raw. But my other two beautiful children, my rainbow babies, keep me grounded. I cherish every memory I was able to make with Laura and I would do it all again. I imagine my two precious angels watching over us and I hope to make them proud of their Mumma.

Someone once said to me that you have to have a sense of optimism to decide to bring a child into the world. I'm not sure if it is optimism that I feel but I do know that my family does not feel complete. I don't want this to be the end of our story. Hopefully there is another rainbow baby in our future.

    Jacinta Gould - Canberra, ACT Australia

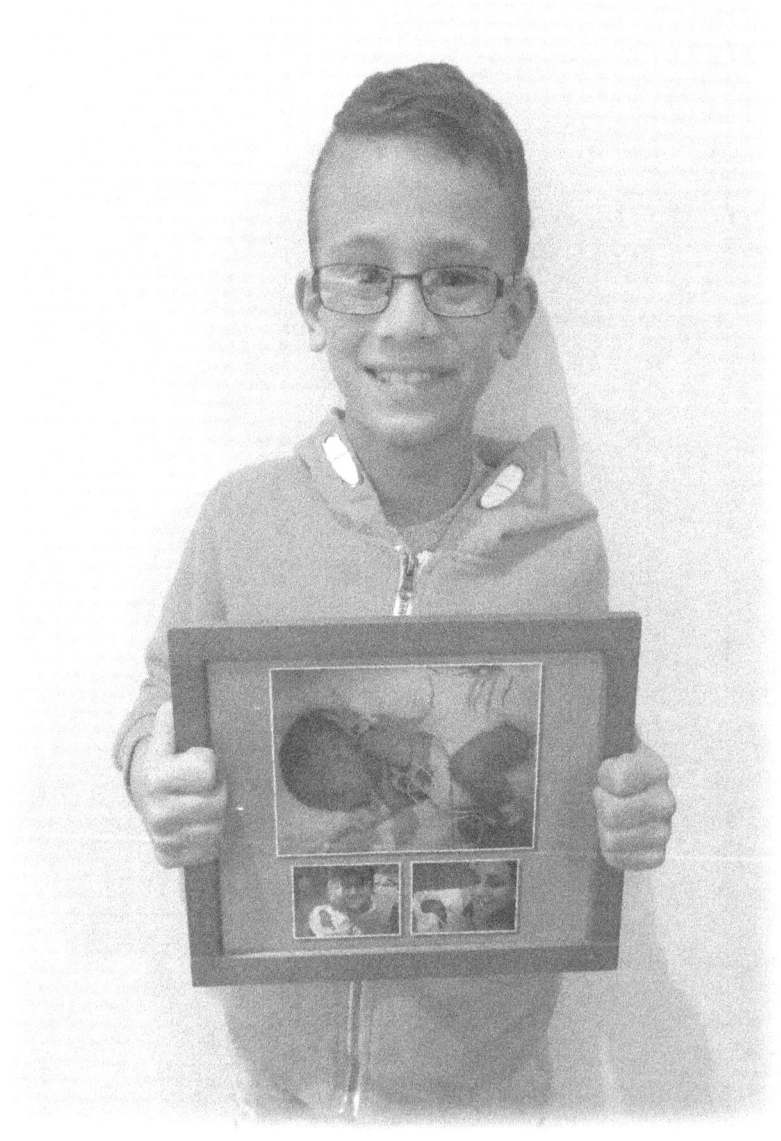

"Our emotions were everywhere! We questioned every moment; was our baby going to be OK mentally and physically? Did I let our baby down by not nourishing our baby properly?"

Jayden James

Before I begin my story, I'd like to start by mentioning my two sisters who have both experienced pregnancy complications and miscarriage, including the coordinator of this book, Melissa. I admire and respect her for giving the women who have generously opened their hearts to contribute to this book, the chance to express themselves and to hopefully feel some sort of closure in sharing these beautiful and inspiring stories.

Although I have not experienced the loss of a pregnancy, I have known the difficult feelings and the emotional roller coaster associated with premature childbirth. Experiencing my sister's heartbreak of miscarriage and stillbirth and trying to comfort and support her when not knowing what to do. Then there were feelings of anticipation and worry, when my twin sister also experienced premature labour not long after I did. Not knowing what the outcome will be is quite daunting.

My husband and I had been in a relationship for over five years before we married. We decided to try to start a family soon after our wedding. In the first month of trying, a positive test result came up on a home pregnancy test. I had a few symptoms so I went to the doctor's for a blood test. Hormone levels were low at 22, so the doctor advised me to do another test within 48 hours and it dropped to 10.

Within the week I had an extremely horrible and painful period, which is unusual for me. The doctor explained that I might have had a very early miscarriage. I felt quite disappointed, and was confused about what had happened.

We tried the next two months with no positive results. By the third month I fell pregnant with all the signs and symptoms and a strong hormone level. Pregnancy was well on its way with all of the expected appointments with my obstetrician.

Morning sickness set in until 16 weeks. Cravings of heavy food like pasta and burgers became normal for me.
Although I was growing, my belly wasn't growing as big as the usual size at each gestational period.

At 31 weeks my obstetrician noticed no change in growth from my 28-week check-up. He seemed concerned and requested an extra scan done by another specialist to measure the baby's growth. Of course I felt very nervous and scared: would my baby be OK? My obstetrician booked me in to have several check-ups at the hospital to monitor the baby's heart rate. He wanted me to have steroid injections to prepare the baby's lungs in case of an early delivery. I did this for the next two weeks. He told us our baby had stopped growing at 28 weeks.

By the 33rd week of my pregnancy, I was beginning to have Braxton Hicks contractions. I went to the hospital for my usual check-up that afternoon. The nurses set me up and kept checking the baby's heart rate. I asked if everything was OK, as the heart seemed very low. I was beginning to understand how these machines worked so I was concerned. The nurse explained that I was actually having contractions and the baby seemed a little bit stressed. They called the obstetrician and he ordered another steroid shot and asked me to stay overnight for observation. I knew something was not right by this stage. I called my husband and he stayed the night with me. I didn't get any sleep as I was attached to monitors all night.

The next morning at 7am, I received a phone call from our obstetrician. He explained to me that sometimes in situations like mine, the placenta decided to die prematurely. He said that sometimes it's safer to take the baby out earlier rather than keeping the baby inside the womb where it was not being fed and growing properly. He told us that we were going to be parents that morning!
A midwife came to speak to us about the possibilities of our child not surviving. I had hope and I knew that my baby was going to be OK.

My husband and I were excited but so scared at the same time. We both had no idea what to expect. Our emotions were everywhere! We questioned every moment; was our baby going to be OK mentally and physically? Did I let our baby down by not nourishing our baby properly? I had done everything by the book when it came to my pregnancy.

At 8.30am on 23rd August 2007, I was given a spinal block and our beautiful son Jayden James was born by emergency caesarian.
All I wanted to hear was his first cry. When he let out a loud scream I felt such relief. But Jayden was born very tiny - he weighed 1.3kg. He was so tiny and so precious.

He could breathe on his own, but he was just too small to be out of the Special Care Nursery. He needed to grow and he slept in the humid crib for three weeks. He was tube fed my breast milk. I was nicknamed "Daisy" in the NICU because I had an almost endless supply of milk! I guess it was meant to be, because my beautiful boy needed as much nourishment as he could get.
Each day, he improved with a few little scares along the way. I was so proud. We were so proud.

The nurses had let me stay in hospital for five days so I could bond with him while I was recovering. When the day came for me to have to leave Jayden at the hospital, I was a wreck. I wasn't supposed to go home without him. It was an unsettling feeling. I broke down and cried. But then I realised he would be in his own cot in our home before too long. We had to be patient.

I visited him every day, being dropped off and picked up while still recovering from the caesarian section. Funnily enough, I forgot about the pain I was in. I was just focused on getting our boy home. I was in my own world. I felt like the only people in my world were my son and I. I didn't realise this until he was home. A mother's instinct I guess. Although I had support of my husband and family, my main focus was Jayden.

After a long three weeks, Jayden was allowed to sleep in a cot, still in the NICU. We were so happy! He was putting on weight and getting stronger. Another week in the NICU and he was allowed to come home! Finally! This was one of our happiest moments.

I am so blessed that we were given such a precious miracle in our life. Jayden is now nine years old and he is a wonderful child. These hard times were also an amazing learning time for us. They made us stronger and helped us appreciate life so much more.

I respect each and every one of the women who has contributed to this book, for sharing your stories. Writing and sharing can be good ways to find closure. And to the precious Angels that are not with us on earth, you will always be in our hearts.

Rebecca Riggio - Sydney Australia

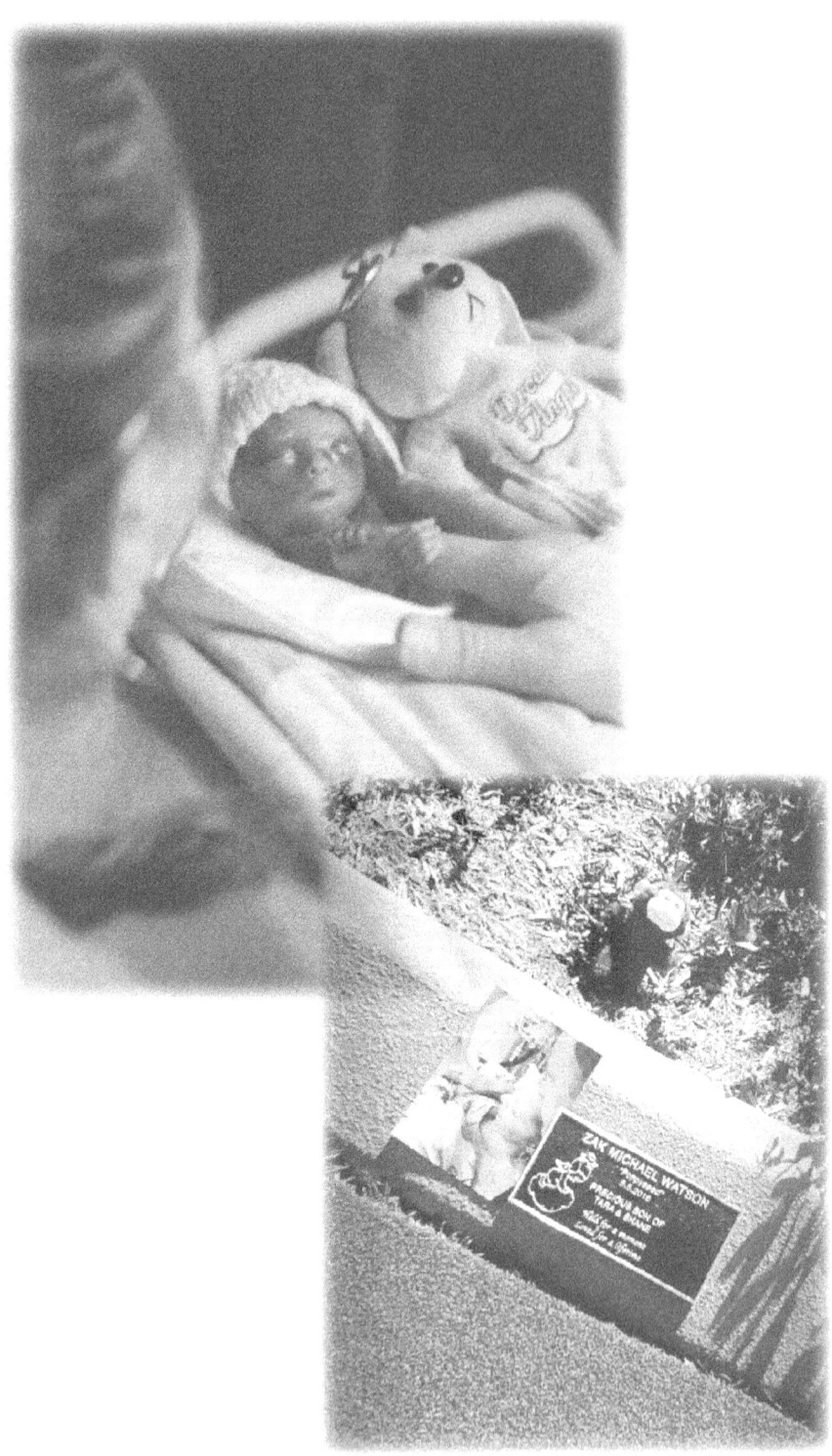

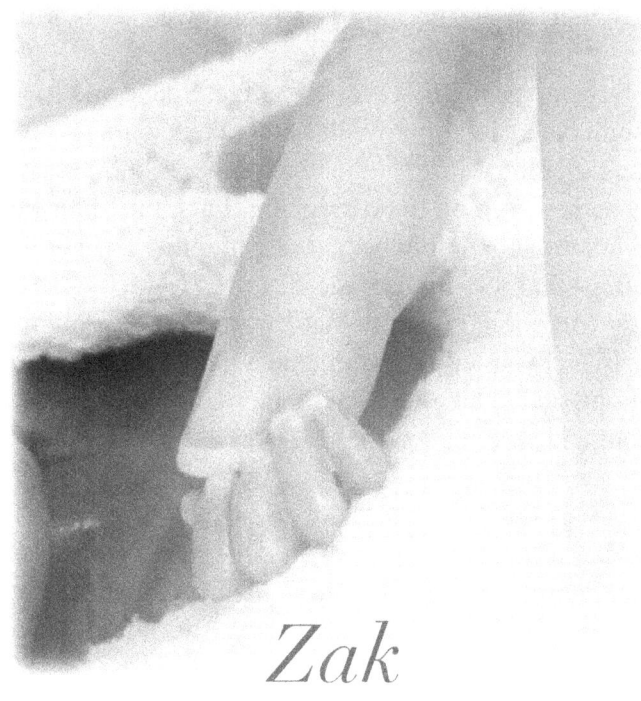

Zak

A letter to Angel Gowns Australia

I was recently a recipient of one of your beautiful wraps for my baby that was born at 22 weeks & three days. I wanted to share my story with you and my heartfelt thank you for what you do.

My story is long, so I apologise in advance. But please know that what you did for myself, my partner and my baby will never be forgotten.

Every part of me feels that I need to write this: for me, for Zak, for our families, for any of Zak's brothers and sisters that may come, for even one other person that this may help. In knowing that, it's impossible to know when or how to start.

It's been just over one month since he was born; a little longer than we knew what we were facing. I could say it was the day our world changed forever, but there's been so many of those days. My world changed so many times, because Poppyseed was my world.

It was 29 December; my first world change. Shane and I were on our way somewhere and that week I had taken so many pregnancy tests it was ridiculous! I remember each time telling Shane I was barren; I was never going to be pregnant. Each time he would laugh at me and tell me it had only been a few months! Being pregnant, being a mum - that was it, that was all I ever wanted to be and I never knew with more certainty that I wanted to be a mummy to Shane's babies. I wanted to give Shane a baby that he could tuck in every night, and spoil every day; that would know that daddy adored them and would adore daddy. Because that's what Shane deserved.

So on that day I took another one - and this time there was a line! So faint but definitely a line. This was the first thing I learnt: positive tests don't come with two dark lines! I went into the kitchen and messaged Shane who was waiting outside in the car - he needed to come back upstairs. I told him I thought it was positive but it's so faint. We stared at it. We needed to know for sure so we went straight to the shops and bought a digital one. No interpreting lines; it would be a yes or no!

I took the test and put it on the bench. The little clock icon flashed for an eternity. I walked away; Shane stood staring at it. And then my world changed. It says "yes" he said. That was it - Poppyseed was on the way. I kissed Shane and then all the thoughts of what our baby was going to look like, all the things we would do together as a family and the images of being a mum rushed through my mind. That moment was so precious.

The next months were uneventful. Poppyseed was perfect. No morning sickness. No symptoms - just this beautiful feeling of growing our baby. I know for sure that I felt Poppyseed move at 11 weeks - pure love. I spent every moment from then focusing on feeling our baby.

At 12 weeks we had our first photoshoot. Our baby was real and was incredible. Poppyseed was a wriggler! After some photos I asked if I could hear our baby. That sound - it's like nothing I had ever heard before. Strong, steady, calming.

Again, weeks went by uneventfully. We were in our second trimester now and of course that meant we were out of the danger stage. This was lesson number two: when you are pregnant, you are never out of the danger stage. Everyone and anyone could now know that we were having a perfect little baby! I would have shouted it from the rooftops if I could have, but I settled with telling everyone I knew. I planned maternity leave, day care, swim school and the nursery. Poppyseed would have it all.

I loved being pregnant, loved it. I slept like a trooper, and napped most days. I went off meat and had to often bargain with Shane on a suitable amount of meat that I would eat at dinner time. I would have my hand on my belly all the time, sometimes just to try and feel Poppyseed; other times to say, hey baby, I know you are in there and I love you. Daddy would talk to Poppyseed too. Those moments, when I think back, still make me smile and bring tears. Daddy would tell Poppyseed all the things they were going to do together, would tell Poppyseed to be good and to look after me. Daddy even sung to Poppyseed. It was the three of us and we were just living the most perfect life.

Time grew closer to find out the sex. Anyone that knows me knows I'm a planner. There wasn't a chance I was leaving that appointment without knowing whether our baby was a girl or a boy. As we grew closer, the suspense was overwhelming and the days were so long. I swore all along it was a girl and Shane agreed. Girls are everywhere in both our families and we were going to be hard pressed to change this.

About a week before I remember a clear feeling that Poppyseed was a boy. And I was so sorry for all those months I had called him a girl and for his pretty girly nickname!! Daddy wasn't convinced.

April 20 came. We went to our appointment and again saw beautiful pictures of our baby. Poppyseed was unstoppable with wiggles. So many photos and measurements were taken. There was a strong beautiful heartbeat. And then we asked - I think I saw it before Alison (our sonographer) said, let me show you. Poppyseed is a boy!

I had no idea what I was going to do with a boy; but I could not have been happier. I still remember Shane's words: I can make boys! I had my two boys and in that moment I could not have loved them any more. That was the happiest moment of my life; another day my world changed.

We made everyone wait. I wanted to photograph our reveal and my beautiful photographer was on the way to our house that night. Shane wasn't so keen, but I remember saying, this might be the only bubby we have and I will regret it if I don't have these photos. Only now I realise how profound that was, and how much those photos now mean to me. The smiles, the happiness and the love that can be seen in those photos I will cherish forever.

While we waited I was in a daze. We were going to have a baby boy! Shane would have to do the toilet training because you know, he had the equipment! I was going to dress him in suspenders and all kinds of adorable boys' clothes, and his dad was going to save him from this. Shane looked up AFL onesies; our baby was going to love AFL, just like his dad. That's exactly why the very first toy Poppyseed ever had was the football, bought as soon as we knew our baby was on the way.

That night we took pictures and shared the news with our family and friends. Poppyseed was a boy! I fell asleep that night with a smile on my face. My two boys - the world was just as it should be.

The next lesson was the hardest - the fall, from the highest of highs to the absolutely lowest of lows. Without knowing, that very next day was another day my world changed.

My phone rang while I was at work. It was the doctor's surgery, telling me my doctor wanted me to come in and the earliest appointment they had was just after 1pm. Everyone knows that's not good. Shane and I convinced ourselves that it was related to the position of my placenta and because of that I went to the appointment alone. The first one I ever did or would do without Shane.

When I arrived our wonderful doctor took me straight in - another bad sign - you never don't wait for the doctor. He began to tell me that something is abnormal with bubby's brain. I can't tell you much, we need another scan, it will be OK, we will get the scan done and go from there. I had only heard the first line. I called Shane while I was walking to my car. Holding the report in my hand, I tried to explain through tears and trying to breathe.

I sent him the report with the big words and we began Googling. Somehow we managed to convince ourselves it was common and it was all going to be cleared up at the next scan. Of course it was.

That weekend was a long weekend. It meant an extra painful day until the next scan. It consumed my every thought at that point and all of me willed for it to be OK. I'd give anything, I'd do anything to make my little boy OK.

April 26th came and we arrived at the 2nd level ultrasound. Our specialist started measuring: perfect arms, perfect legs, perfect fingers, perfect toes, perfect hands, perfect eyes, nose, face, perfect. It wasn't possible for anything to be wrong, when he was so perfect in every other way. Poppyseed was especially cheeky today - he would continue to flip when she walked away to confuse her. He hid his left ankle and then shortly after would only show his left ankle. To this day these remain some of our best memories of our little boy and his cheeky personality.

Then she said, I can see what they were looking at in his brain. My heart broke again; this wasn't going to be the outcome we had convinced ourselves of. We were led into a consultation room, big words were said, pictures were drawn and the world just became a blur. Nothing made sense and there were no answers. We need to do an MRI, she told us. This meant more waiting and days of despair. I think I knew then that this wasn't going to be the happy ending I so badly wanted.

That night I told Shane I was going to have a shower. He was going to call his mum and I thought he would be busy and I could be loud in the shower and not worry him. I sat in the bottom of the shower and I just cried. A moment later, there was Shane fully clothed in the shower holding me. Shane and I spoke about the choice we might have to make, but in the end there was no choice. I knew I would rather live a lifetime in pain than have my baby go through a moment of it. I'm so truly grateful that Shane and I were always on the same page, often without words.

I don't quite remember where it fits in the story, but I remember one night finding a story so similar to ours (although I didn't know this at the time). It was written by a lady outlining what she had experienced. Hers was much shorter than mine! As I read it I cried; it was only reading her story that it hit me. If this was bad, I was going to have to go through labour. Now I'm a smart person, but for the life of me I had no idea why I didn't realise this earlier. I turned to Shane and tried to tell him what I had just realised. I said, "If this is bad I'm going to have to..." I couldn't finish. He said "… give birth; I know, baby." He had already realised this.

Shane didn't think reading was a good idea; but I know that it was. It was because of that story that I got through. That story gave me the steps of what I was going to endure. I knew before every step what was going to come next. I will be forever grateful to that woman for sharing her story.

April 29 came, the day of our MRI. It was a Friday and we had already been told that any scans wouldn't be looked at until the specialist came to the hospital on Tuesday. Another impossible wait. As I lay there in the machine with my headphones on, I thought, "Where are Poppyseed's headphones?" I kept saying to myself - hoping it meant Poppyseed heard it - it's OK baby, don't be scared baby, I love you, over and over again.

Shane and I drove home. Drives to and from the hospital were mostly silent now. Just lost in our thoughts. Shane went to work and I went to bed. Then my phone rang; it was our specialist. She told me that we needed to come back straight away. She said the scans were "bad, really bad", and they didn't need to wait until Tuesday to review them.

I rang Shane and he came straight home. I was talking to my family, updating them and I remember hearing Shane cry. I had never seen or heard this incredible man break like that and I rushed off the phone to comfort him. Shane and I managed so far to take it in turns. On the days that he struggled, I was strong and on the far more frequent days I struggled, he was strong.

We made the silent drive to the hospital again. This was the point at which we became "famous" at the hospital. No more waiting rooms, no more explaining our story; we said my name and we were constantly and immediately ushered through. I remember joking that it must be really bad. I joked a lot - I still do because it helps.

The midwife told us our baby's brain was "wild". That was the word she used - "wild". Then our specialist came in and asked if we would like to see the scan. Of course I did. I needed to know what everyone was looking at; I needed to see, to understand. She explained that where bubby's brain should be, this had significantly degraded and bubby had very little grey matter remaining. A "catastrophic insult" was what she called it. None of that made sense. I was healthy, I had taken my pregnancy vitamins, I had not eaten anything I wasn't supposed to. I had done it all "right". Stats like 1 in 100,000 were discussed; stories like only ever seeing it one other time in a young girl who was in a horrific car accident - still none of it made sense.

The outcome for our Poppyseed was horrific: seizures, disability, no intellect, unknown impact on his physical abilities. She said, do you need time to talk about it? Shane and I looked at each other and at the same time we said we didn't. That's one of the things I'm grateful for in this whole thing. For me there was no choice; the choice was made for us.

What followed was paperwork to sign, appointments made, more paperwork. Questions about whether we wanted photos, handprints, footprints. I just wanted my baby. I signed everything, completely in a daze. There would be a birth certificate, we were told, and a death certificate. We would have to arrange a funeral. For any birth over 20 weeks this is a legal requirement. This was all new learnings for us. We had one question: would our baby be born alive? "We don't know," was the answer. "Possibly, possibly not, but if he was, it wouldn't be for long."

The social worker came in. As a social worker myself that was always going to be interesting. She told me I needed to take my "social work" hat off and put my "mum" hat on. I remember thinking - and later told Shane - I can't do that. My "social work" hat was the only thing keeping me in that room, processing and understanding the choices I was making. Without that hat, the mum in me would have fallen apart.

After being told about payments we would be entitled to, and what seemed like a lot of talking without taking a breath, we were allowed to go home. I was still carrying and feeling my baby, but I knew that I had just signed his little life away. I just kept telling him I was sorry, telling him I loved him.

Shane said to me a few days, maybe weeks, later, "That was the day we lost our son." That was the day he was taken from us. And he is right. What came next was just steps along the way.

That day I cried. I felt guilt and felt hopeless. But the next day I decided that my baby was not going to spend the last few days feeling nothing but my despair. He didn't deserve that. He had done nothing wrong. He made us the happiest we had ever been. So we went about having a beautiful weekend together, just the three of us. Of course we were destroyed and heartbroken, but we did our best to talk to him, to laugh about him, to make him have his last few days as happy ones. I was helpless, but I could do that for him.

On Sunday we went in to start the medication. This was just a quick trip in, take the meds, monitor for an hour and then go home again. It was relatively uneventful. At the time the tablet was handed to me I burst into tears. I knew as soon as I took this it was over, it was real. The nurse began to cry as well. Immediately I felt guilty! But she held my hand, said some beautiful words and after the hour asked if she could hug me as I left. I could never turn down a hug.

The next day was Labour Day. Ironic, I know. After hours and several calls to the birth suite, at 3:30pm we were told to come in. They had tried to bring us in when it was quiet and put us in a room semi out of the way; all these things they had to consider for us. We got to the hospital, my family and Shane's parents.

Shane and I were led to the room we would be in. There was a butterfly on the door. This seemed to confuse the reception lady and she doubled checked with the midwife that we were supposed to be in that room. When she left I asked the midwife if the butterfly meant something. "Yes," she said, "it's our subtle way of saying what's going on in the room." "Not very subtle!" I laughed. And later reflected that I didn't know if I should be insulted. At 5 and a 1/2 months that poor lady thought I was full term! Too many cakes and sweets that were blamed on Poppyseed!

The Friday before, the day we signed away our baby, we were told the process. The medication on the Saturday would ensure that it would be quick; in the time that they had followed this procedure no-one had gone over 48 hours. We would be admitted and then they would start two tablets every four hours for five rounds. After a 12-hour break, it was the same process. That should be it. OK, my "social work" hat understood that.

So we went through the first round, again uneventful, nothing happened.

During this time, every midwife was beautiful; everyone one of them reassured me, cared for us both and made me feel like I was in capable hands.

We were asked to pick a beautiful hand-sewn blanket that Poppyseed could be wrapped in, that we could then keep. Daddy chose one with cars on it, but he had bonded with one midwife over AFL so she chose one with soccer balls on it and told us to have both. She showed us the beautiful hand-sewn wrap that Poppyseed would be placed in; this too we could keep. It was made from donated wedding dresses by a foundation called Angel Gowns Australia - who knew these wonderful people existed? We were shown the little beanie and the tiny booties that he would be dressed in.

We were shown the beautiful memory box we would go home with. Families that had experienced what we were going through donated these. Ours had a little girl's name on it and we agreed instantly that one day we would do this for Poppyseed too.

We were told that professional photographers would come after the birth and take photos for us; anything we wanted, anything we needed.

Of course we wanted nothing but to take our baby home, but there's no doubt that the amazing memories that we received, the love and care that was paid and the time we had together that was captured helped ease some of that pain.

After the first 12-hour break, we went again, medication every four hours, five rounds - and again nothing. With everything that had happened to us, of course I was going to break this record too. Then the review came and a suggestion that I was going to be sent home before starting the whole process again from the beginning. I refused. I was not going home; I was not leaving. I didn't want a rest.

Luckily for me the specialist stepped in and told the doctors to give me another one of the tablets I took on the Sunday and go again. This time the number of tablets in the four hour rounds was doubled. The outcome for Poppyseed was known; now it was time to get me through it. I apologised to her for ruining her 48-hour stat; we laughed.

So we went again - another tablet and another round. Slowly things started to happen. Very slowly. A side effect of the tablets is high temp, so I spent a 12-hour period with a temperature of 39.5. I had constant blood tests to make sure I hadn't contracted an infection. I had smashed their 48-hour time frame.

Another 12-hour rest and the forth round was started. Finally things started to move. Contractions started coming and we just had to wait for my cervix to get to 5cm so my water could be broken. After that happened it would go quick they told me. I didn't believe them.

At one point the pain was so excruciating I said to Shane, "I can't do this, I want to go home". He just rubbed my back, gave me my 10,000th jug of ice and told me I could. They asked me if I wanted an epidural. I said no. I had all my choices and all my control taken away from me; I was about to lose my baby - but I had this choice, I could decide this and I had control. I settled for morphine and gas.

It kept running through my head: Tara your baby is going to be tiny, Tara your baby is not going to be alive, Tara you will have to say goodbye, Tara you won't get to take your baby home. Over and over as if trying to convince myself; trying to prepare myself.

My waters were finally broken, and they were right, things moved quickly, or maybe they didn't. Shane would have to answer that because what comes next is hazy for me at best.

I asked Shane, with extreme pressure below and the desire to push, how will I know when I should? Shane asked the midwife. "She will know," she said. I didn't. I had never done this before. I had no idea what I was doing.

A point came when I just couldn't help but push and with one, Shane told me he could see his head. The midwife told me he was coming and with just one more push he would be here. Again my mantra, a final push and I knew he was here because the relief was instant; no more pain.

At 1:40pm on 5 May, Zak, our beautiful baby was born at 22 weeks and three days. He never took a breath. He never opened his eyes. And most importantly he never had a second of pain. Daddy cut his umbilical cord and he was handed to me.

He is perfect, he said, he is absolutely perfect. And he was. I don't know why, (probably due to drugs!) but at that point I was calm, the physical pain was over, we had done what we needed to do. I was holding my baby. Shane was overcome and cried. I held him and told him it was OK.

I later found out the midwife that delivered Zak had her own experiences at 22 weeks and 27 weeks. I had so much admiration for this woman, to keep doing what she does. But I was so glad she was there; she really knew how I was feeling, she really understood. She laughed when we laughed, she joked when we did, she cried when we cried (when he was born), she was angry when we were angry. She said all the things I needed to hear as a woman who had just become a mother. She knew and I'm forever grateful.

I held him. I looked at him, trying to take in every detail, trying to figure out his features. He had my face - round - and my eyes - big and round. That was where I ended. He had his daddy's nose and lips; he had his daddy's long lean body type. He had perfect fingers and toes, long legs and massive feet. He had perfect little ears and fingernails and toenails. He was beautiful.

Our families came in; I was never going to force anyone, but he was there for cuddles if they wanted. All of them did. We have photos and we cherish these. He felt all of their love.

I wasn't done quite yet though. It became apparent a while later that I must have retained some placenta and surgery would be required to stop my constant bleeding. It was estimated at a minimum I had lost approximately 1.3 litres. And after a quick faint in the shower I was rushed into emergency surgery. I had forms to sign, consent for a hysterectomy, acknowledging that I may die. I was wheeled out, looking at Shane holding Zak and I thought, this is it, he is going to lose his son and me in the same night and I couldn't bear to think about what that would do to him. I told Shane I loved him as tears ran down my face, and I told him to look after our son.

As they put me to sleep my calmness left me and I burst into tears. I don't know who she was, but at that point a lady reached down grabbed my hand and told me I was going to be OK. That was the last thing I remembered.

I woke up and was wheeled back to Shane and Zak. Shane later told me that about 2.5 hours had passed. I had missed Zak's bath because the photographers couldn't wait, but they had plenty of photos of it for me. We have since received the professional photos and there are some truly beautiful ones of me holding my son and of the three of us together. Thankfully we have these photos, because my memory of these being taken is non-existent. I don't remember it at all. Shane says they wheeled me back and instantly began taking photos. They did a wonderful job.

There are photos of Shane and Zak, and in hindsight I'm so glad he got that time with his son, just the two of them. I had so much time with Poppyseed; just him and me, and I'm glad they got their time too.

Shane and I decided early on that we didn't want to prolong our time with Zak. We wanted to remember him being perfect and we knew that as time went on this would affect his little body. Although it wasn't part of the plan, we soon both agreed to have him overnight with us. He was placed in a special crib with a cool pad on the bottom. He couldn't be beside me because the crib required constant power; but from my bed I could see him wrapped in his wrap on his blanket and I could feel him with us.

In the morning we said our goodbyes. We were both scared to lift him, but at the last moment I asked the midwife to lift him - I wanted to kiss him one more time. We were told Zak could be brought back to us at any time, that he wouldn't leave the ward until we left the hospital. But we knew that was the last time we would see him.

Zak went with so many things: his football of course, his two jumpsuits - one saying "I love Mummy" the other "I love Daddy" - and matching socks, three blankets - one from Mummy, one knitted by Grandma, and one brought by Nani (wherever he was going he was going to be warm!) - a teddy from Nani, and a teddy from his three cousins that he would never meet, but loved him dearly. He went with Mummy's t-shirt that had Daddy's blue handprints on from his gender reveal. He went with the bracelet that Daddy had made for Mummy. He went with all the love that his mum and dad had for each other and for him.

After several more days and a late night medical emergency call, I had decided I was ready to go home. It had almost been a week in hospital and I was being woken for monitoring constantly, including a standing heart rate every hour, even throughout the night. I asked the nurse what I had to do to go home. She gave me a list - lists I can do - within 24 hours I had checked this off.

Mother's Day arrived. I was going home; I had had enough. We waited patiently for the doctor and at 3pm she arrived. I was signed off and the next step was here - to leave the hospital without my baby. Instead of my baby I had flowers in my hand and I was wheeled out to the pick-up bay. I again told Zak I was sorry and I loved him. As Shane drove us home tears ran down my face.

The next few days were a blur. We arranged the funeral and it was as beautiful as it could be. There were moments that were just so surreal. Questions that we never thought we would have to answer. And from then until now, we take it a day at a time.

There are moments that I'm overwhelmed with emotions, like the day his birth certificate arrived, or the one where his room decals came, or the one where I opened his death certificate, with cause of death listed as "Open Lip Bilateral Schizencephaly". But I am comforted by words that were said at Zak's funeral. Even if we knew why, even if there were answers this wouldn't take away our pain and this wouldn't make it any easier.

I am incredibly firm in my belief that it is my job to be strong for my son. I am his mum and that's my job. And more than anything I am adamant that my son will not be remembered with just tears and heartbreak. He brought us so much joy, so much happiness, and he deserves for his memory to bring us laughter and smiles. That's something else I can do for him.

People have struggled to know how to help, to know how to respond. This I understand. But in response to this I say: for the short moment it is hard to say anything, it is a million times harder for us to breathe or to function. I want my son acknowledged, I want to talk about him, for the world to realise he existed. For his memory to be strong; anything else to me is just not acceptable. There is nothing anyone can say to make it better and there's nothing anyone can ask me that I haven't already answered, so there's no fear of upsetting me. If all else fails, just a hug, an "I'm sorry for your loss" - that's all that is needed and it truly means the world.

To Zak, my beautiful baby boy. I will love you for a lifetime, every day. I now have no fear of my time ending, because that will be the day I see you again. Until then I will miss you every day. I am so sorry I couldn't help you; but I hope you hear me every night when I go to sleep and see me every morning when I place your blanket on Daddy's and my pillow. You will always be my first baby and you will never be forgotten.

To Shane, there are no words to thank you. You are my strength everyday; you are the reason I'm breathing. You are my everything. I'm so sorry you had to go through this pain, but I will spend my lifetime making all your dreams come true, like you do for me.

To the midwives at RBWH, thank you for all your love and care, for Shane and me and but mostly for our Zak. You are truly amazing people and what you did for us made the impossible bearable. I will remember each of you forever.

To Angel Gowns Australia, thank you for existing. Thank you for giving us something beautiful to put our baby in and dressing him so beautifully. I will be grateful for that forever.

To Precious Wings, thank you for our memory box. Thank you for filling my hands with something to take home and for giving us precious memories to remember our baby. To the beautiful family who lost their baby and dedicated their box, thank you - we know your pain and your gift eased ours. We too will buy a box in memory of Zak one day.

To Heartfelt, the incredible photographers that came that night. The day our photos arrived was a happy one. Thank you, without you I would not have memories of my baby's first bath or pictures of my boys together. What you have given us is priceless.

To our family and friends, thank you is not enough; we will never be able to repay the love and care you have given us. Thank you for loving me, and thank you even more for loving my son.

To any other mother that goes through anything like this, I know your pain. I've felt it. It does lift and you are not alone. You are strong, stronger than you ever thought you would need to be - stronger than anyone should ever have to be. Just breathe. I promise it gets easier.

Tara Roulston - Everton Park QLD

An angel in the book of life wrote down my baby's birth, and whispered as She closed the book,
"Too Beautiful for Earth".

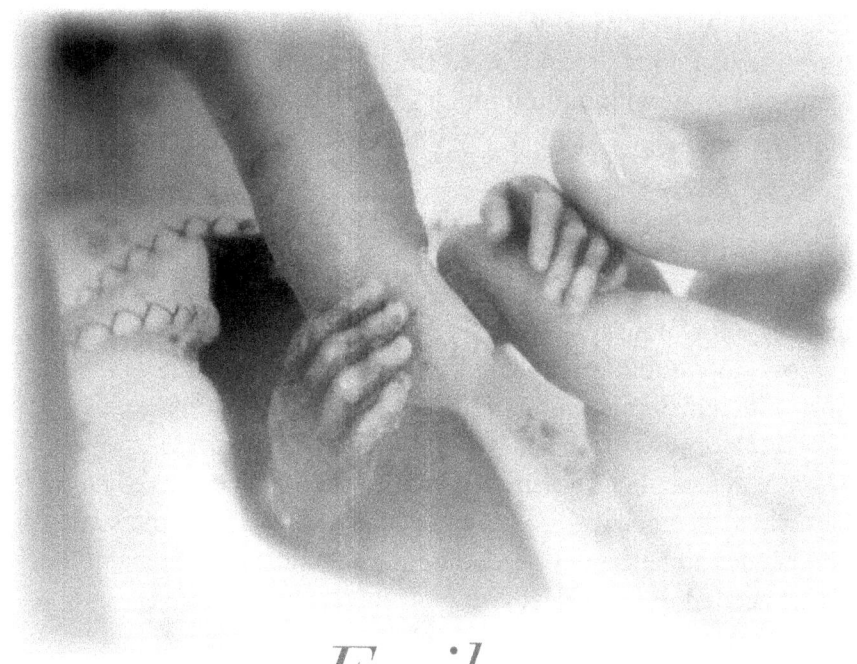

Emilee

"This isn't the type of thing that happens to me."
"You hear of other people going through this, but I'm not one of those women."
"This isn't real. This wasn't supposed to happen."

I lost count of how many different ways I had said the same thing. I'd heard of stillbirth, of course. But stillbirth wasn't supposed to happen to me.

It was when my midwife started exchanging awkward glances with the other midwife in the room, I realised I'd repeated the same phrase over and again… and again. It was time for me to stop talking.

I was 20 weeks and four days pregnant. I'd been in hospital for four days. Every ultrasound had shown a healthy baby - our third baby girl. Every check with the Doppler had given us a healthy heartbeat to listen to. But last night things had changed. My bleeding had gotten even worse. Small contraction-like feelings came and went with building intensity. I put my prayers out to the universe and hoped like hell my little girl would hold on.

I'd even looked at the clock at 11:11 and knew it must be a positive sign.
"We think you should call your husband to come back up," they'd told me a few hours earlier, after labour was obvious. And here he now stood, holding my hand, as he had my other labours. This time with a different kind of tension. He wasn't letting go.

"Have you thought of a name?" We had to name her? We had to name her. She needed to know she'd been loved from the start. She needed to belong. I needed her to belong. And for that to happen, I needed to let her, let go.

"Emilee. But with two e's." And unlike any time we'd had a similar conversation before, Michael agreed immediately.

"I think it's time, Carolyn. It's time to deliver your little girl," my midwife, Karen, said gently. "When you're ready. But it's time to meet her."

I'm not sure what I was expecting, but to me, at that time, the pain was just as intense as either of my other labours. I needed to rock. I needed to kneel up. I needed to feel like I was in a 'proper' labour. Physically, the relief at the end was the same too. The difference was the agonising silence. No crying baby. No congratulatory sayings. No pats on the back for the happy dad.

Karen, who two weeks earlier had been a stranger, now became one of the most significant people in our world. As she placed our tiny bundle on my chest and asked Michael if he wanted to cut the umbilical cord, she put her hand on me and told us how beautiful our daughter was. Over the next few hours, she ensured that we made as many memories as a family as possible. She knew what words to say and guided us in what to say to others. She took photos and footprints. And her care with our little girl was always gentle and precious. I truly believe that our experience in hospital would've been completely different if not for her by our side.

The next day and a half was a blur. Emilee stayed with us the whole time. Confusion set in and I found I didn't really know how to act. I wanted to hold her as much as possible, but was that weird? I wanted to put her in the cot while I slept or went to the bathroom, but did that mean I didn't want to hold her? I could hear the motor of the cold cot running. How did that make me feel? The midwives had put a little gown on her and I thought it was ugly. Was that ridiculous? I needed to put a blanket over her body. But was that to make me feel better or to stop visitors from looking at her?

As family came and went, I felt numb. I didn't want to grieve in front of some of them. Others didn't want to grieve in front of me. Lots of whispering happened around me. And I let it. Michael, my mum and my sister filtered calls, made the important decisions and got me ready to leave hospital - without Emilee - to come home with one less daughter.

For a long time after her birth, the moment we walked out that door and left Emilee in the arms of Karen, was the hardest. The next hardest was leaving the cemetery on the day of her funeral. I felt like I was walking away on her. As silly as it sounds, in those moments, I felt like I was betraying her.

Our life was different now. I thought of life in two stages: Before Emilee and after Emilee. I felt worried rather than excited when I heard other people were pregnant. I often felt like I had to force myself to be happy – or at least not to show sadness (and mostly because it made other people feel bad). And we spoke about death with our girls – often.

If there's anything in this whole process that I feel proud of, it's the way we have dealt with the loss with Jasmine and Ava. From meeting their sister in a cold hospital room, to involving them in the funeral arrangements by choosing their favourite coloured balloons, to asking a thousand times why Emilee couldn't stay with us, we have been nothing but honest with them.

I think that many people often disregard how resilient children can be. We are proud that we are raising two girls who look at death sensitively, realistically and with a genuine sense of how long forever is.

For a long time after Emilee's stillbirth, Jasmine, nearly four at the time, asked questions constantly. She missed her baby sister with a love that she couldn't understand. She wanted to know why the doctors couldn't make her better, why she couldn't stay in Mummy's tummy and still now, is very perceptive when people around her are upset.

I am also proud of the way Ava, then 18 months (now five), pulls me up when talking about our family members. One of the trickiest questions I get asked is "How many children do you have?"... Well, obviously I have three but to the person who only knows me with two, or the person I've just met, or someone I haven't seen for a while – do I really need to go into our story? If Ava is with me – yes I do. Otherwise, she corrects me. She freely talks about her little sister and tells people that Mummy had a baby that died. She draws pictures for Emilee. Tells her new friends about her and includes her name on things like raffle tickets and Melbourne Cup sweeps!

February 23 is the most emotional day of our year. On her first birthday, we wanted to remember Emilee appropriately and I really wanted it to be perfect. I had planned to have a picnic, release a rainbow of balloons and spend the day peacefully. Just as it did the day of her funeral, it poured with rain. So the picnic was out, the balloons didn't fly into the sky and we ended up heading in to the local shopping centre and playing arcade games with noisy teenagers. It tore me apart and I hated it.

I realised afterwards that I had put too much emphasis on it being perfect. I realised it wasn't going to be the perfect day I wanted it to be, without Emilee to blow out the candles. We decided then that Emilee's birthday would become our 'Family Day'. So we make it a day the girls will remember. Whether it's roller-skating, ferry rides, trips to Luna Park, chocolate and pancakes for dinner, or playing in the park, we plan to always fondly remember the day that Emilee came to us. There is the rest of the year to be upset that she didn't get to stay – but her birthday – that's for fun!

Shortly before Emilee's birth, I had begun making personalised candles for family and friends and the day before I was admitted to hospital, I had completed my first order for a perfect stranger, thanks to the world of Facebook. In the weeks after Emilee's birth, my inbox slowly filled with new orders and I began to immerse myself in choosing the right wording, the correct ribbon colour and embellishments so that I could create something special for other people. The candles were for christenings and weddings – special milestones that I would never be able to celebrate with my little girl.

Creating the candles gave me space. Michael would take the girls away while I worked, or I worked while the girls were in childcare and school. My music played and I created special keepsakes. And I cried – even when I was excited to have a new project. It became my therapy. It also became my serendipity. Something that almost felt like it was meant to be, but could only be because I'd lost Emilee.

> *"Serendipity: the effect by which one accidentally stumbles upon something fortunate...*
> *Especially while looking for something entirely unrelated"*

From these first orders, a business grew – Serendipity Event Candles. The next couple of years were consumed with creating candles and other personalised items to help create special memories for other families. Before long, our home was so cluttered with candles and all the paraphernalia that went along with it that we decided to move to a bigger house so that we could give my business the best shot. It had changed from my therapy to trying to make money. Outwardly I was confident. I attended wedding expos, advertised locally and set up a website, deciding to build a business for myself, my family and in memory of our baby girl. Running the business gave me confidence and the strength that I needed to show everyone I was coping. It was also nerve-racking. With every few steps forward, I'd fall back a little, trying to perfect my product because it was a reflection on me. On Emilee's memory.

Serendipity Event Candles was getting to the stage where I couldn't cope with the workload and started to look into hiring help. It was now taking so much of my time that it also needed to prove itself financially. This is where it ended. In a way that I found difficult to explain to others, the guilt that I had with the business overwhelmed me.

One night, sitting down to about a dozen different projects and applying for a new wedding expo, I fell to pieces and realised why I hadn't pushed my business growth earlier. I was making money off Emilee's stillbirth. As serendipitous as I had been treating it, I realised that I had felt guilt in benefiting from her death. And I couldn't cope with that.

All at once, relief took over. I realised I no longer needed Serendipity Event Candles. I had begun to resent endless phone calls with customers who insisted the print wasn't right or I'd used the wrong font or the ribbon was a shade too dark. My grief had come to a point where I didn't need all this. I was ready to close that door. Start a new chapter. I had worked through the most difficult part of my grief with my hands, and they were now going to be able to rest. I had kept myself so busy and would now be able to spend more time with my girls and cherish them that little bit more. And that was where I needed to be in that moment. In a similar way to Emilee's birth, it was time for me to let that part of my grief go.

Fast forward and you'll find us here – just over four years After Emilee. Life is tough and everyone has their struggles. This is ours. It makes us who we are. Our little blessing has taught us resilience; has taught us that life doesn't always make sense and we don't always find out the answers. Loss changes you and that's OK. So it should. We didn't get here without hard work.

We find courage where we need it, love in those around us, and comfort in each other.

Emilee will always be a part of our story. We have promised each other nothing less.

        Carolyn Viera - Sydney, Australia

"Broken, I headed to the beach and stood atop a cliff, icy wind whipping my hair, staring at the aqua ocean eroding the surface rock, feeling like grief was eroding my heart. I didn't know what to do with all of that sadness. I gave my baby the name 'Aspen Lee', and that day, laid her to rest in my mind on the coastline of South Australia."

Seven Angels...
Sette Angeli

I am the mother of seven Angels in heaven and 10 Earth Angels (eight beautiful boys and two gorgeous girls!).

My journey as a mother began in 1988 when I delivered a healthy son. Two years later, in 1990, his brother would follow. The following year I had my first miscarriage but I didn't know it at the time. It was only in falling very ill and having a cyst rupture on my ovary just shortly after that an infection was discovered in my uterus caused by an incomplete miscarriage. It seemed like the loss of 'Baby Gabriel' was the beginning of something. I was in the midst of a bitter and messy marriage breakup and not sure how to feel about this loss. I wanted to grieve, but I found it so hard to cry for a baby I didn't even know I was having. It would be years later that I would be able to honour that loss and the space he/she left in my life.

In 1994 I would be blessed with another son, and two years later I would endure another miscarriage – this time at 16 weeks. I was in Adelaide, and away from my other children who I was missing desperately. I was unable to fly and heartbroken to miss my second born son's sixth birthday. I had started to bleed and was sent for an ultrasound that detected no heartbeat and a foetus too small for dates. The sonographer quizzed me, asking, "Could you have miscarried and fallen pregnant again?" I had no idea why she was asking or what this could mean. I told her that that wasn't possible and she simply blurted out, "I had a woman in here just before you who is 10 weeks pregnant and her baby is much bigger than yours." I was mortified. How could she be so cruel? I continued to bleed and that was that. I was sent in for a D&C, four days after the ultrasound – the waiting was hard, and yet part of me didn't want it to be over; I didn't want to say goodbye, I wasn't ready.

The hospital staff put me in the maternity wing and I had to endure listening to the newborns cry while I waited to be taken to surgery. It was torture – a cruel and unusual punishment for a grieving mother to endure. A young mum walked past carrying her baby and I couldn't help but stare as she walked away. My dream was shattered, but she held her dream in her arms. Life can be so unfair!

Broken, I headed to the beach and stood atop a cliff, icy wind whipping my hair, staring at the aqua ocean eroding the surface rock, feeling like grief was eroding my heart. I didn't know what to do with all of that sadness. I gave my baby the name 'Aspen Lee', and that day, laid her to rest in my mind on the coastline of South Australia. Primal sobs escaped my heart all the way home in the car. Then I poured all of the pain into a journal, into poetry, and into writing for the now defunct grief newsletter Pen Parents of Australia – Candlelight Magazine. For seven years I worked tirelessly with them to counsel other grieving parents, to share my story and my poetry. Little did I know rough times were not over for me yet.

I was blessed in 1997 to welcome a daughter and another son two years after her (1999) and 18 months later another daughter (in 2000). But in my quest to have more children, there would be more losses – in 2002 a miscarriage (Willow) then another baby boy born in 2003, another son arrived in 2004, and then three miscarriages followed consecutively in one year (Ash, Jael & Rowan).

In October 2005, I was admitted to hospital for yet another D&C. My body wasn't giving this baby up. The hardest part of this one had been that my baby had a heartbeat, but it was too small for dates. My OBGYN counselled me to make a decision – if nature wasn't going to run its course, or if my body wasn't going to relinquish and expel this baby, then I needed to abort. I went to the Sunshine Coast for the weekend and prayed that I wouldn't have to make that decision; that I would be spared that agony, and thankfully, I was. By the time I returned for a follow-up ultrasound there was no heartbeat. The decision was made.

After that, my OBGYN wrote to my GP and said, "Meekehleh's baby-making career is over!" So hurt and disgusted by the way he chose to word my desire to have a family, I called him and complained bitterly. He told me that although I was not yet 40 my body was acting like it was and I wasn't likely to ever have another healthy baby. I knew that I could prove him wrong.

In 2007 when I was delivered of another healthy son, I sent that OBGYN a birth announcement with a note: "Here's the healthy baby you said I'd never have!" My ninth child, and my first ever c-section. There and then I came to the conclusion that I was done. I had managed it. I was blessed. I was grateful. I could breathe out. My family was complete! All of those miscarriages had taken their toll. I was mentally and emotionally exhausted, and knew that I could not do it all again. I was at university and beginning a new journey in my life - studying nursing so that I could become a midwife and support other women who, like me, had struggled through the milestones of pregnancy. I understood that overpowering urge to become a mother against all odds.

Once more, I changed my mind, and again I went on a quest to add to my family. Unfortunately in 2009 I lost yet another baby (Sam). I was beyond shattered and had to deal with yet another incompetent sonographer with zero compassion.

How can they say lightning doesn't strike twice in the same place? That's just not a legitimate quote; at least, it isn't for me. But now I was obsessed with wanting another child. I was yearning and I wanted to fulfill that need. For several months I was denied the result I so desperately wanted, so I decided that if the test was negative one more time, I was giving up.

That month the test was blessedly positive, with exactly the same due date as the baby I lost in 2009 (Feb 25), and we had a road trip planned from Brisbane to Sydney with six children in tow. I hoped all would be well and I clung to a thin veil of hope. Two days after we arrived in New South Wales, I started spotting and decided that was that, there would be no more babies for me – I was done. I figured heaven was proving to me that there was no more joy here for me.

To my surprise the pregnancy continued, but not without drama. I was hospitalized from 31 weeks for bed rest because I was dilating and they feared an imminent arrival. And then my baby's heart rate was flat. He just didn't seem to be doing well inside. I was induced two weeks early and thankfully was able to have a VBAC, despite being in a high-risk category I had wonderful staff and I was really looked after well. But my little boy's heart rate was still not satisfactory and I saw the worried look on the doctor's face. He told me all I needed to know. It seemed like this wasn't to be my happily ever after at all. However, my tenth child arrived on the tenth of the month, 13.5 hours after I was induced. He was healthy and well. I had done it!

But by the time he was one month old he had fallen very ill, and would remain so until just before his first birthday. I nursed him back to health, after enduring one of the worst years of my entire life. He is now five and has just started school. He is perfect and beautiful and amazing, as are all my children.

Despite these trials, I am one blessed mama. I am forever grateful that despite 17 pregnancies in total more than half ended well, even when I had babies that ended up in special care.

Grief taught me a lot about myself. It taught me that it cracks you wide open and exposes you to people and things you wouldn't usually have experienced. It showed me the best and worst of people. It made me scared and vulnerable. I felt weak at times. I felt sad that my body couldn't just do what it was supposed to do – what it was designed for. I felt like a failure. I felt lost. And it's really hard for someone else to stand in the space of grief with you when they haven't endured what you have. It's really easy for someone else to say "It wasn't meant to be!" or "Don't worry, you'll have another baby!"

But the 'what ifs' and the lack of understanding are the things that hurt the most.

Grief is indefinable. It is different for everyone. And if you've never been through it, you cannot truly understand it. Trying to describe it is a little like trying to tell someone what the bitterness of a lemon tastes like when they've never tasted one. 'The Grief Club' is not a club you ever want to join – it's not a club you can ever leave. While, for me, time has dulled the sadness somewhat, and I have 10 beautiful children to enjoy, as well as one grandchild now, my seven Angels are never forgotten. I celebrate their lives on one specific day throughout the year, rather than seven different days, which would just drag out the sorrow. They each have a bauble with their names on for the Christmas tree, and I have framed plaques for each of them - because naming them honoured them, and was an acknowledgment that they are part of my family, and always will be.

I think of them and I celebrate being their mama. I am grateful for each little Angel, who I hope to someday meet…knowing that greeting will be bittersweet, and thanking them for being part of my life, no matter how short our time together was.

    Meekehleh Maree Connors - Hunter Valley, NSW Australia
                  www.meekehlehsbooks.com

The Moment Our Family Became Stronger

After having five healthy full-term pregnancies to my ex-husband, I was excited when I fell pregnant to my current partner. We had met just months before we found out and were both over the moon as he had two kids from a previous partner that he saw every second weekend.

It was February when I had the usual symptoms and took a pregnancy test to confirm it. I had some spotting but the doctor said all was good. Things were going great!

I had done something to my back so my doctor prescribed a strong painkiller (Panadeine forte), which I had never taken in other pregnancies. He said it was safe for the baby; I wasn't too sure but figured he knew what he was talking about.

I had one ultrasound at the X-ray clinic and, because I had accidentally double-booked, one at the local hospital 10 days later.
The first scan showed a healthy baby boy, everything was perfect. Then I went to the hospital scan not thinking anything bad was going to happen.

The sonographer seemed to be looking for something. I have had enough scans to know what they are measuring and looking for, and I knew right then that something was wrong. I said to her, "There's no heartbeat, is there?" She said, "I just have to get my supervisor." This new person came in and just put her hand on my arm and didn't say anything. I said, "There isn't any heartbeat is there? So what do we do now?"

They asked me to come back on Monday - it was Friday - and they would do a repeat scan. We went home and broke it to all the kids and family that there was a chance that I would be going to hospital on Monday and not coming home that night. The kids were devastated and so were we.

On Monday I had my bag packed ready to go. We arrived at 8am ready for the scan. It was confirmed that our baby boy had grown his Angel wings. So I went in to 'mum mode' or robot mode. I said, "OK, now what happens?" They sat us in a little room with three chairs and a little table with a box of tissues on it. My partner, Ben, looked at it and said to me. "This is weird," and I had to agree with him. Eventually the social worker came and spoke to us. She said we had to go to the delivery room and get things going.

They inserted a tablet to bring on the labour and they put us in the observation room as the other room they had was soundproof, had a TV and a double bed - but a young girl was in there with her mum as she was losing twins. We said, "It's OK she needs the room more than us." I got a few niggles but nothing serious so I ate my dinner and Ben's dinner as well. I shouldn't have done that because the pains got worse so I called for the gas. There was no way I wanted to feel this if I didn't have my boy to keep. I ended up vomiting from the gas, first time ever that has happened to me!

At 9pm on 27 June, 2011 our baby boy was born still inside the amniotic sack. I was 22 weeks pregnant and he was perfect. I got to hold him and the nurse asked Ben if we had any names yet. We didn't but Ben chose to name him Robert Edward Buckley after his friends, and it was also a family name. Ben went home to the kids after a while but I kept Robert with me until the next day. We had decided not to let the kids see him as they were at that time aged between four and 12 years old. They got to see photos of him that the nurse took the next day, but he was starting to deteriorate by then as he had passed up to 10 days earlier so he had absorbed some of the fluid.

I said my goodbyes to Robert but still hadn't shed a tear. I had to be strong for the rest of the family. We came home and started planning the funeral, we decided on a cremation. It was a small event with a couple of family members there. I still didn't cry.

Fast forward to November 2011, near to Robert's due date, and I started to feel sick. I thought it must have been thoughts of Robert; but I thought I'd take a few pregnancy tests anyway. They were all negative but I had all the familiar symptoms. I think all up I took six tests. On Robert's due date – 4 November - I took another one. I was pregnant! We decided not to say anything until I was 12 weeks.

The pregnancy loss coordinator who helped us was amazing with the loss of Robert and rang me to let us know the autopsy results. There was no known cause of death. I joked around with Ben and said, "Your mum wanted him more than we did," as his mum had passed three years earlier. A couple of years later I found out her actual time and date of passing. It was 9pm, on 27 June, 2008. The same time and date as Robert's passing but three years earlier! I had instant goose bumps and said to Ben, "See, I told you!"

When I was 12 weeks pregnant with this new baby we decided to tell everyone, which happened to fall on Christmas Day and the whole family was there which was good.

On 3 January, 2012 I had a Down syndrome screening ultrasound done at a private clinic. When we got there we were excited. Then the nurse said, "I'm sorry, there is no heartbeat."
I said, "You have to be kidding me, right?" I did everything right this time. I cried and cried. I cried for Robert and I cried for Tad (that's the nickname we had for him as we didn't know what sex he was yet). I told Ben I was sorry but he said he was sorry. We both felt guilty and like failures.

We came home and told the kids and their response was, "Not again!" This time I had to see my GP on the way home and he told me to ring the early pregnancy loss clinic. They told me that I could wait and my body would miscarry but it could be up to six weeks or they could book me in. I told them that I had delivered a stillborn six months earlier and if this baby had passed away then I wanted it out of me NOW! So I had a D&C done. I asked them to do testing to see if Ben and I were compatible to have a child together and the reply was yes. We also found out Tad was a boy and we had lost him to Down Syndrome.

Because of my losses I want to get into the pregnancy loss sector. I want to help others get through what we have been through. I want to let others know that it does get better.

Since losing my boys I have completed a diploma in management and I have completed a diploma in community services. Hopefully one day my dream job will become available.

Ben didn't want to try and have another baby. It totally broke him losing the boys. The kids had to go to grief counselling as my middle boy was showing aggression at school and saying hurtful things. It came out in the counselling that he felt it was his fault they died because he hugged me too tight. I explained that it wasn't and he has come a long way since then and doesn't get in to trouble as much anymore. The kids have coped really well with what they have been through and they miss their baby brothers but it's brought us closer together as a family. It has made us stronger.

I have found out what my dream job is called, it's a bereavement doula and I can't wait to be able to help other families in their time of need.

Dani Milward - Ningi, QLD

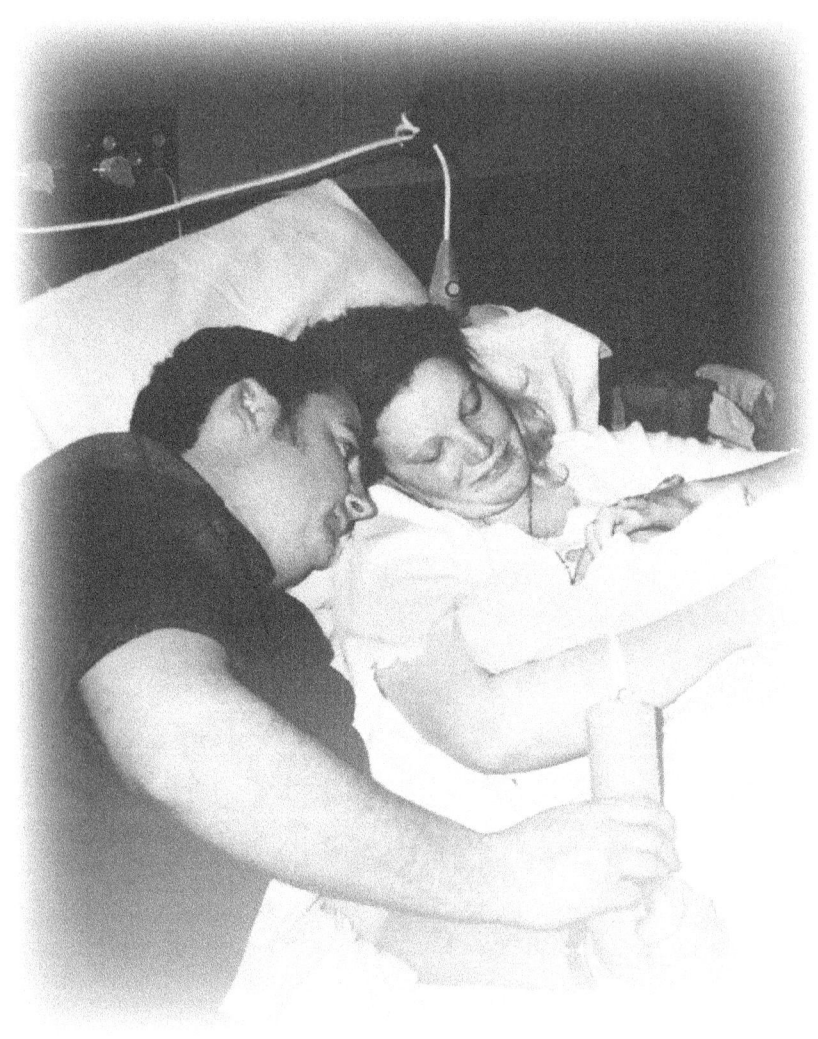

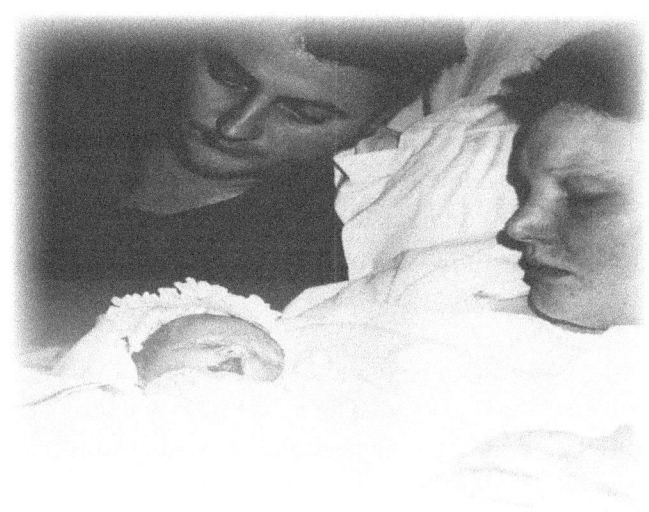

Chaunté Rose

Today I think back to what happened on this day, 18 years ago. Many don't know as it has always been a difficult memory to share, but today I do it with an amazing strength, understanding and a new faith.

On the 24th July 1998, I presented to the local hospital Emergency department with pains that the Doctor in charge was concerned enough about to send me to the closest maternity hospital. He was worried I was suffering from a placental bleed.

After organizing care for our oldest daughter (thanks Nanna & Poppa Cormack) and being taken to the larger hospital by our sister in law (thanks Mandy), we were met there by my parents (thanks Mum & Dad).

After many tries at getting blood, which they never obtained and with them not being able to do any further ultrasonic testing as no one was available at 8pm, we were brushed off with no concern and I returned home later that evening.

Life continued for the next week. Playgroup, shopping, even a visit to the Adelaide Entertainment Centre to see Disney on Ice with our 3-year-old daughter. The weekend came and the weekend passed. I pushed aside the fact that I hadn't felt movement and that our baby was settling down to come four weeks early.
I had been told that 'old wives tale' many times that weekend and thought at 21, other women knew much more than me and it must be true!

Monday 3rd of August arrived and I was happy that I had prepared our Nursery over the weekend. The all white cot, linen, bassinet and furniture that would be the peaceful, tranquil room for our new baby to rest and grow in.

That afternoon I called my mum at work and just wanted to tell her that I felt the baby was going to be here sooner rather than later. "Why is that?" She questioned me, "Are you in labour?" "No, I just haven't felt the baby move for a while and you know what they say, it must be settling down before its arrival". Then I felt my mum become uneasy and she asked me to ring our private OB/GYN Doctor. I tried, but he was out of the office and the receptionist asked us to ring the local hospital. Under their advice I told my now husband, Phillip, that I needed to go to the hospital. So off we went with our daughter and thought this may be the day we became parents again and our daughter became a big sister. Dopplers were used to hear the heartbeat.

Nurses entered and exited the room continually. Monitors were placed on my tummy and continually moved. Baby cries were heard in other rooms. Phillip held my hand and Courtney got super excited. The nurses' faces started to look concerned. Phone calls to our Doctor were being made. "Doctors at the golf course" we are told, "but he's not concerned. He will come in to check on you when he's finished". "We have a heartbeat, so baby is doing ok, it's just a little slower than normal" the nurse told us. "We will keep the monitor on and see how baby goes". I start to worry, but Phillip reassures me it will all be OK.

"What is your normal heart rate?" Questions the nurse. "Around 80-90, quite high". "Hmmm. I think we can hear the baby's heartbeat, but it is sitting around 90 also. We know it's not yours, but we will give the doctor a call again". Minutes passed and the nurse enters with a trolley and says "We need to prep you for an emergency caesarean. The doctor will be here as soon as he can, but he's worried the babies heart rate is getting too low". Tears. Disbelief. Anger. Fear. All these feelings and many more envelope me and I start to think how I didn't want a caesarean and how this is not what I planned.

Well I can now say – Pregnancy doesn't always go to plan!!! I ask if they can just let me deliver naturally, but they calmly explain that they need to perform the caesarean to save our babies life. In that moment I totally agree with them.

Family arrived at the hospital as Phillip had started calling them to tell them our baby would be here in minutes and not hours as I was being rushed in for an emergency caesarean. I was already in the theatre with the theatre staff, still waiting for the Doctor to arrive. I keep telling myself whilst rubbing my tummy "I'll get to meet you soon, won't be long now". The cannula is inserted. The IV is connected. The gas mask is placed. Phillip is holding my hand. I'm asked to count backwards from 10. I stare at the large theatre light. It looks like a flying saucer. I'm counting.

Darkness.

Eyes open. It's bright. I'm excited.

Everyone is around my bed. I'm still in the theatre. No one is excited. No one is smiling. I look at Phillip to my left, sitting on the little wheelie stool he was sitting on when I went under the anesthetic. "What did we have? Where's the baby?" He can't talk and his eyes are red. Oh wow, I think to myself; he's been crying because he's so excited to be a daddy, that's so sweet. He still can't talk. The nurse brings over our baby, all wrapped up snug in those pastel fleecy hospital blankets that we are all too familiar with. I can't wait to meet our baby. I'm so excited. Yippee! I can't wait to cuddle our baby. Woohoo, "Tell me what we had!" I say to Phillip again.

The nurse arrives at my side in between Phillip and I to lean in and show me the baby. "You had a baby girl. But unfortunately she died. I'm so sorry". WHAT! Is this a dream? C'mon, wake up now Rachel. This is ridiculous. Dreams when you're under anesthetic are crazy. WAKE UP NOW RACHEL!!! NOW!!! I close my eyes. I really close my eyes and then open them again! Nope, everyone still looks the same. It's not a dream. The baby girl I'm looking at is dead. [As I write that line, I've just burst into tears and my chest is aching.] I feel exactly as I did 18 years ago when I finally got to meet our precious daughter ~ Chaunte Rose. Stillborn - without breath – at 35 weeks. 3rd August 1998, our lives changed forever.

I could write about how the next 18 years played out, but I won't bore you with our lives. But I can say, it is our lives and we live it each and every day. She is always in our hearts. She is always in our thoughts. She will always be our daughter. This is now our life.

When you ask how many children I have, I will tell you "I have five children; four live with us and our daughter, Chaunte, is in Heaven". It may be confronting for you, and make you feel awkward; but this is now our life.

"Well you can always have more children". Yes, we did, but not one of our children can ever replace Chaunte or fill the hole in our hearts; but this is now our life.

"Well you have other children to keep you busy" you may say. I smile and say "Yes I have been blessed with four other beautiful children", but I want to say "Which one of your children could you live without?" But this is now our life.

"Maybe there was something wrong with her. Maybe you're better off with her dying when she was a baby". REALLY!!! Yes, we did have an autopsy performed on our purely, perfect, precious baby girl. Guess what – she was perfect and had no abnormalities at all.

She was in perfect health prior to dying in utero; but this is now our life.

"Maybe it was meant to be. God had a better plan for her!" Hmmm. No, he is all loving and would never intentionally cause this much pain in anyone; but this is now our life.

The diagnosis for her passing was a massive Fetal-Maternal Transfusion. Chaunte had passed away four days prior to her delivery. It wasn't Chaunte's heartbeat they were monitoring; it was mine. Nothing I did, nothing she did, nothing God did; nothing caused this to happen. It is not something that is routinely tested for in pregnancy at any stage. The only sign of it occurring is decreased and eventually no fetal movement.

If our daughter was delivered when we first presented to the local hospital Emergency Department and on the same night, the closest Maternity Hospital, I can say our baby girl would be with us today. Would she be fully functioning? I can't say. She may have been on life support and lived a life of challenges, but she would still have been loved and supported. She may have been perfectly healthy and in her final year at high school. She would have been through kindy, primary school, her Year 11 Formal; she may even have a boyfriend.

We never got to celebrate these milestones in her and our lives; but this is now our life. We will never get to help guide her in her life and watch her develop into a beautiful, independent woman like her older sister. We will never get to see if her younger sisters and brother are just like her or see them loving each other. We will never see her graduate from further studies; whatever career she may have chosen. We will never get to meet her chosen partner and experience the grand gesture of her future husband asking her father if he can take her hand in marriage.
I will never go wedding dress shopping with her and help her plan her perfect day when she marries the man of her dreams; that we call our son. Her father will never get to walk her down the aisle to be married to that man we call our son. We will never get to hold and look after her babies – our grandchildren – yes we've also

missed out on their lives also. They will never get to come to Nan & Pop's house for sleepovers and continual spoiling.

Our parents, family and friends have also missed out on these magical moments; but this is now our life. Some people think we should be over it by now. Some people think we shouldn't have the need to still talk about it. Some people think we should focus on what we have and not what we have lost. Some people feel the need to have an opinion on how we, as bereaved parents, should feel. But luckily it's not your life; but this is now our life!

Having to plan a Funeral for your baby is one of the most awful tasks I have ever had to undertake. What coffin would you LIKE or would you LIKE the cheaper option of a material covered box? What colour flowers would you LIKE? What would you LIKE to dress your baby in? Is there anything special you would LIKE to place in her coffin? Where would you LIKE to hold the Service? Would you prefer a burial or cremation? What cemetery would you LIKE to have your baby buried in? What burial marker would you LIKE to order? I'd LIKE to never have to bury my baby.

I would never want anyone to know how this feels, every second of every day of every year, for all our lives. But this is now our life.

Please acknowledge our daughter, sister, granddaughter, niece and friend. I would rather hear her name than be in fear to mention her name. It makes us know she is in your hearts and thoughts.

Stillborn babies are still our babies. The impact they have had and continue to have on our lives is tremendous and everlasting. Six babies are stillborn every day in Australia. The statistics for stillbirth are not improving. One in four pregnancies ends in loss – I have been pregnant 16 times and have four live children – it's very accurate I guess. We are part of these statistics and it breaks our heart.

Rachel Windsor-Cormack- Adelaide, Australia
Chaunté Rose Foundation

Trials and Tribulations

At 38 years old, this is my fifth and final pregnancy. I have one living child. My husband and I long for another baby, a sibling for our son. But at our age and with our history, our financial and emotional resources are depleted. We need to start thinking about saving for retirement, and those funds have been depleted in our efforts to have a family.

I am seven weeks along and lying on the table as the ultrasound technician searches around for a heartbeat. It is all too familiar to me, the silence except for the typing as she clicks here and there and measures this and that. She says the pregnancy is too small to see trans-abdominally (the ultrasound probe on the tummy with the gel that you see in all the movies). So, I will need to go empty my bladder. I just drank a ton of water and I've been suffering for the past hour, needing to pee. So I follow the routine; I am always too small at this stage to see the baby from the outside. I go to the bathroom and return for the trans-vaginal. I'll spare you the details

189

of that. More silence, more clicking. More seconds ticking by. I've known I am pregnant for three weeks now and it all comes down to this second. Is there a heartbeat or not?

I didn't see my first pregnancy on ultrasound. I miscarried very early in my first trimester. It was as if my monthly cycle was just a few weeks late and I had a heavy period. Less than 20 per cent of pregnancies end in miscarriage. But when you think about it, that is a lot of pregnancies ending early. After a heartbeat is detected, that risk falls to 3 per cent.

There wasn't much concern at this point about me not being able to have a healthy baby. You know, many women experience early miscarriage. The body is very smart that way. If there is something wrong with the development of the baby, the body knows that. The stars need to align. It is quite a miracle to get past the first trimester. That is why most people wait to announce their pregnancy until they are "safe". I didn't know it at the time, but I did eventually find out that there is no "safe zone" for me.

The second pregnancy, I was further along in my first trimester. I was spotting, and didn't feel the typical early pregnancy symptoms. So I went in for an early ultrasound and there was no heartbeat. I remember the doctor being called in and he said he was sorry. He wanted to just get another doctor to look and confirm his findings. The other doctor took a look and said how very sorry he was. I was sad about the loss. I was starting to become worried that I could not carry a baby to term. The doctor advised me that they don't really investigate further until there are three early losses.

A couple of years later, I hadn't conceived again. Now it was time to investigate the dreaded infertility problem. I had a tubal dye study done to make sure my tubes weren't blocked. Turns out, the dye wasn't getting through one of the tubes. But I still had the other one. I had an exploratory procedure done called a laparoscopy. They go in with a camera through two small incisions in my abdomen to look around at my reproductive system. Other than some scar tissue, which they cleared, everything looked good in and around my uterus. The doctor put me on a drug called clomid. It didn't work. I didn't want to go down the road further into the infertility treatments. My husband and I decided to see what the future held and not worry about it. We believe in God, and we believed that we would have children if it was meant to be.

Fast forward almost eight years. We hadn't been actively trying or worried about having a baby. Just as I had prepared myself for the real possibility that we may be a childless couple, I got a BFP. That is pregnancy talk for "big fat positive".

I spotted early on with my third pregnancy, and I had several ultrasounds. At around 14 weeks, I was standing with my work group and felt a gush of blood. Luckily, I was wearing a pad and saved myself some huge embarrassment. An ultrasound revealed that the baby was developing splendidly, and there was no explanation for the bleed. Some women just bleed throughout pregnancy, they said. My 20-week ultrasound was normal. We did not want to find out the gender. We were looking for a surprise. Boy, did we get one, but not in the way we were expecting.

At 24 weeks, I started spotting. I had a sensation that the baby was kicking straight down. I joked with my sister, "He can't break out of here, can he?" I went to the emergency room one Saturday night at exactly 24 weeks. They listened to the heartbeat and sent me home. They said to follow up with my doctor on Monday. The spotting stopped and I felt fine by Monday. The nurse called and left me a message. She heard that I had been in the ER, and if I felt that they should take a look, I could come in for an ultrasound. I felt silly at this point. I mean, I had been spotting my entire pregnancy. There was a heartbeat. I felt like I was being an over-worried pain in the butt to my doctor. I did not go in, a decision I came to regret.

Exactly one week later, on Saturday night, my husband and I went to bed at midnight. We had been up late preparing the nursery for our little one. We went to the craft store and painted little animal plaques for the wall. We painted the room and set up the furniture. It was quite an accomplishment. I was feeling extremely sore and tired, but assumed it was from all the painting. I had to go to the bathroom, but every time I tried, nothing would come out. Finally, I fell asleep. Two hours later, at 2 am, I got up again to go to the bathroom. I felt a gush and my waters broke all over my bathroom floor.

My son was born that night, by emergency c-section, at exactly 25 weeks gestation. He weighed 1 pound, 11.5 ounces, and was 12 inches long. Having a 25-week micro-preemie is a story in and of itself. In summary, we spent 104 days in the NICU (Neonatal Intensive Care Unit), including an ambulance transport to and from a major metropolitan area for heart surgery involving complications. Due to his extremely underdeveloped lungs, he was on home oxygen for the first few years of his life. We gave him nebuliser treatments frequently. It is fair to say that we have been sleep deprived for the past four and a half years.

When my son was almost two years old, he became critically ill with a respiratory infection. He was airlifted to Children's Hospital in Minneapolis, where he spent six weeks on a ventilator. His lungs were unable to oxygenate his blood so he had to go on a lung bypass machine called ECMO. He was on ECMO only four days when he began bleeding out and was rushed into emergency surgery to repair an ulcer.

My son has been within seconds of death so many times in his short life. I believed in God before my son was born, but if I had any doubt in the existence of miracles, that is completely gone now. I know for a fact that Jesus held my boy in his healing hands and gave him comfort and healing during his ordeal. I felt Him. I know beyond a reasonable doubt that my son is here today due to divine intervention. Finding faith through trauma is another fascinating subject for another story and another time. But this story is not done. Our trauma did not end here.

When my son was three years old, fully recovered from his critical illness and rehabilitated (he had to learn to eat and walk and everything all over again), I found out I was pregnant for the fourth time.

We were ecstatic that we were going to have another child. I went to a high-risk OBGYN this time and was being monitored closely.

One of the ultrasounds showed a growth very near my cervix that was suspected to be a uterine polyp. I was referred to a perinatologist for a stitch (cerclage). The polyp was not reachable for removal and it was decided not to place a cerclage. There was a risk of hitting the polyp and causing hemorrhaging. Since my cervix was long and closed, the recommendation was to keep monitoring me closely. I started Makena, a hormone shot, at 16 weeks. Progesterone is the hormone in this shot, and it helps the body stay pregnant.

At 17.5 weeks, my waters broke. I was placed on complete bed rest. The prognosis was not good, but there was still a chance I could make it to 23 weeks, at which time I would be placed on hospital bed rest and attempts would be made to save the baby. I had no fluid left. At my 19.5-week appointment, my baby had no heartbeat. I was induced, and gave natural birth to my Angel, Isaac David. He is buried in my husband's family cemetery.

We spent a lot of time grieving Isaac's death and then trying to figure out if we would ever try again. We wanted another child. We wanted our son to have a sibling. We definitely did not want to put another child through the NICU experience. We did not want to experience any more loss. Financially, we were spent. We were back in the thought pattern that we would not be having any more children. A year and a half after Isaac, we decided we were going to try one more time. We would give it three cycles. If it was meant to be, it was meant to be. If not, we were content to know that our son was an only child and another baby was not in the plan for us. We got pregnant on the first try.

I cannot describe to you the nervous and sad emotions that come with pregnancy after a loss. On that ultrasound table at seven weeks, my fifth pregnancy revealed a heartbeat. There is a little life growing inside me as I type this story. I don't know how the story will end. I am not optimistic. I am not feeling joy. I was happy to see a heartbeat, but I don't want to share the news with anybody until

I make it to 24 weeks. In the US, 24 weeks (and sometimes 22-23 weeks) is the point that the doctors are willing to take measures to save babies. Until then, I am just waiting. Waiting to see if this baby makes it. Waiting to see blood at any time. Waiting to feel movement. Waiting until the next ultrasound to see if there is progress. Every pain, every twinge, makes me worried that I am losing this baby. Just waiting and praying for a happy ending.

But like I said earlier, there is no "safe zone" for me. I will either have a living, crying baby in my arms or I won't. It isn't up to me to decide.

Jenny Tiernan St. Cloud, Minnesota, USA

Update
On 18 April, 2016, we welcomed a healthy little girl into our family. She was born at 37 weeks and weighed 6lbs, 10.5 ounces. She was 17.75 inches long. We are relieved after a very stressful pregnancy to have our family, now complete.

Photographs by Beautiful Lens Photography

Thank You

From the bottom of my heart, I thank you all for contributing your very heartfelt memoirs.

Thank you Kelly from Millyboo designs for designing the cover of this book; Sally from Sally Kennedy Photography for the beautiful cover photo and Mustafa Johnson from Lolite Media for formatting. I am extremely grateful for generously donating your time and expertise.

You all have made this book come to life and made my dream a reality.

Through the words you have shared, we can all appreciate how vulnerable a pregnancy can be and how precious life really is.

Your memoir's are inspirational. They show courage and strength. They share pain, love, joy and hope.

You have shared your journey's of starting a family, becoming pregnant, sharing the joy and the heartache and realising that not one pregnancy is the same and that not all will go to plan.

Writing has helped me to acknowledge my babies and accept that my life would not be the same had they lived. I wonder every day what it would be like, although I am very grateful to have such beautiful, fun loving boys.

My life now, after writing, has taken me to a new world. And although experiencing the loss of a baby is devastating, being able to tell your own story honestly brings new beginnings.

I hope you have found writing about your journey to be healing and comforting and in some way, it has positively changed your lives too.

        With love,
        Melissa

Support

All organisations relating to pregnancy, babies and infants, have an important role assisting families in getting the best help and support they need when their child falls ill, is born with a disability, born early or has sadly passed away.

Not one of them is more important than the other. They work together in supporting these families.

During the time of my grieving and then starting my own blog a few years ago, I made the decision to donate money to a few different organisations for various reasons.

SIDS Australia – Red Nose Day falls on or around Charlize's anniversary.

Miracle Babies – I was made aware of this organisation when I was in hospital giving birth to Charlize and started an auction to donate money to them.

Angel Babies Foundation – This one was chosen by a member of my Facebook page "In Memory of Charlize" as the recipient of the money from my second charity auction.

Angel Gowns Australia – I donated my wedding dress so babies who have died can be dressed and remembered in a beautiful gown. I donated profits I made from my book to this organisation and have recently become more involved in their events.

There are numerous organisations and people that relate to these causes and offer support. I have listed just a few others. Reach out to these organisations if you need to; they are there to help:

- American Pregnancy loss Association
- Australian Multiple birth Association
- Bears of Hope
- Bonnie Babes Foundation
- Carly-Marie Dudley – Artist
- Center for loss of Multiple Birth
- Centre for Loss Births (CLIMB)
- Genea
- HAND
- Heartfelt
- International Stillbirth Alliance
- IVF Australia
- IVF Support
- Jake Garrett foundation
- Life's Little Treasures
- March of Dimes
- MISS Foundation
- NICU Helping Hands
- Precious Wings
- Raising Children Network
- Return to Zero
- SANDS
- The Compassionate Friends
- The Ectopic Pregnancy Trust
- The Miscarriage Association
- The Stillbirth Foundation
- Tommy's
- Yasminah's Gift of Hope

For updates on my story or this book, you can like my Facebook page - www.Facebook.com/melissadesveauxbooks or visit my website - www.Mylifeofloss.com

Faith makes all things possible

Love makes all things easy

Hope makes all things work

www.ingramcontent.com/pod-product-compliance
Lightning Source LLC
Chambersburg PA
CBHW070610300426
44113CB00010B/1485